HIDDEN HISTORY *of* WABASH COUNTY INDIANA

HIDDEN HISTORY *of* WABASH COUNTY INDIANA

Ron Woodward

THE History PRESS

Published by The History Press
Charleston, SC 29403
www.historypress.net

Front cover: Strongman Robert Printy holding two other performers at the Sells-Floto Circus. *Courtesy of John Lawson.*
Back cover, top: Students at the Treaty School, circa 1890. *Author's collection.*
Back cover, inset: Postcard of the Wabash County Courthouse. *Author's collection.*

First published 2015

Manufactured in the United States

ISBN 978.1.46711.805.7

Library of Congress Control Number: 2015939782

Contents

Introduction

More than forty years ago, I began collecting stories of the rich and varied past of Wabash County. I've gone through newspapers from 1846 to the present, traipsed through over fifty cemeteries, gone through musty old courthouse documents and books, read county histories and talked with countless county residents. I began to share these stories with my students and others interested in the past of Wabash County. As editor of the Wabash County Historical Society and the Wabash County Genealogical Society newsletters—*Peek at the Past* and *Family Branches*—I have been able to reach a larger audience. In turn, I have found out even more history of the county, which lies hidden in the diaries, letters, photographs and lives of Wabash residents.

In 2010, Gladys Harvey and I combined our talents and wrote down *Wabash County Chronicles: Raucous, Quirky & Essential Tales*, printed by The History Press. The general public of Wabash County received the book with open arms. Many of the accounts that Gladys and I had accumulated were left out of that book, and readers who enjoyed it wrote, called and e-mailed asking for more. Well, here it is: *Hidden History of Wabash County*.

This book is a unique look at some of the people who have lived here and events that have transpired since Wabash County came to life in 1835. In the following pages, learn more about Chief LeGros, Frances Slocum, "Wabash" George Mullin, Bob Printy and Tommy R. Miller—each adding his or her own unique history to that of the county. Learn more about the traditions that have made Wabash County what it is today, from making

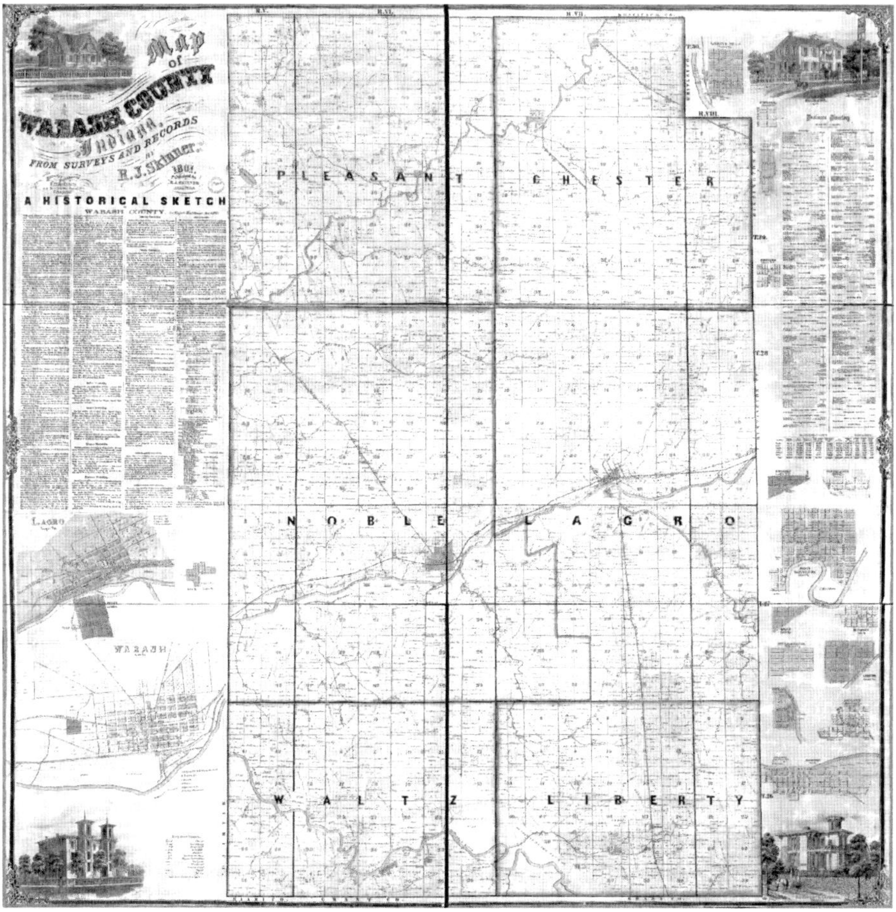

A map of Wabash County, Indiana, 1861. *Courtesy of the Library of Congress, Geography and Map Division.*

maple syrup to the first roller coaster in Indiana, from the Sweet Shop to painting the school ticket booth.

I wish to acknowledge, with my deepest appreciation, the help and assistance my wife, Diana Haley Woodward, has provided. She has graciously allowed me to take over our dining room table to compile this work; she has also been a great help with the computer aspects of preparing this work.

So sit back, relax and enjoy!

Part I
Hidden History of Early Wabash County

Will the Real Chief LeGros Please Stand Up?

Chief LeGros—also known as "LeGris," "Big Body" and "Machekeoltah"—was a Miami Indian who had a village located near the mouth of the Salamonie River where it enters the Wabash River. The town of Lagro, at this site, was named for him. He signed treaties with the United States government in 1795 (the first Treaty of Greenville), 1814, 1818 (the Treaty of St. Mary's) and 1826 (the Treaty of Mississinewa). Several other Indians were known by the same name, and some even lived at the same time, which makes it hard to find the real LeGros.

LeGros was possibly born in the area around Pickawillany, Ohio (present-day Piqua, Ohio), about 1750. His father was also known as LeGros. He had a brother called the "Deer" and a sister who married Little Turtle. In his interview with C.C. Trowbridge, LeGros stated that his family originally came from the St. Joseph's River area. In 1747, Miami chiefs La Demoiselle and LeGros moved their people from Kekionga to the junction of Loramie Creek and the Great Miami River and formed the village of Pickawillany. This village began to rival Kekionga in importance. It also put the Miamis close to British traders, a move that the French feared would ruin their hold on the tribe.

In 1752, the French decided to punish the Miamis of Pickawillany. La Demoiselle's village of more than four hundred inhabitants contained a fortified trading post where British agents traded with the Indian villages of the region. Charles Langlade, who was part French and part Indian, led two hundred French Canadians and Indians in a surprise raid that destroyed the village and trading post. Five British traders were captured and taken to Detroit. LeGros and La Demoiselle were killed. La Demoiselle's heart was ripped out and eaten raw, and his body was boiled and consumed. Pickawillany fell into disuse after its inhabitants were forcibly resettled around Fort Wayne.

LeGros grew up in one of the seven villages that made up Kekionga. His village was located on present-day Spy Run in Fort Wayne. Among the Miamis, a boy officially became a man based on the experiences he had but generally was considered a man at about twenty-five years of age. This means LeGros became a man during the American Revolution. On October 7, 1778, Colonel Hamilton, on his way from Detroit to Vincennes with a force of 177 soldiers and a large body of Indian allies, met with various chiefs at Kekionga. Attending were both a Gris and Gros who gave presents to Colonel Hamilton. Hamilton encouraged them to help him retake Vincennes from George Rogers Clark. It was not recorded if LeGros went with them.

In 1780, Clark's successes emboldened a force of 104 men, mostly of French ancestry under a man name LaBalme, to attack Detroit. Little Turtle and his followers attacked LaBalme at the Aboite River, killing 40 men. Some managed to escape in the darkness, but most of the survivors were captured. Little Turtle was just beginning to earn a reputation as a war chief at this time. LeGros, who was emerging as a "sutle [*sic*] chief and councilor" of the Miamis, accompanied Little Turtle. By 1786, LeGros had emerged as a principal chief of the tribe.

The 1790s was a period known as the "Indian Wars," when the Miamis and other tribes of the Old Northwest fought with the United States government. On October 19, 1790, Little Turtle defeated General Harmer's American forces. Harmer's Defeat, as it was called, took place at present-day Fort Wayne, just a few miles from LeGros' village on Spy Run. One account states that Little Turtle, along with LeGros and Blue Jacket, paraded through the streets of Detroit "uttering yelps while bearing long poles strung with the scalps of many American soldiers." On October 22, five Miami villages in and around Fort Wayne were laid to waste.

On November 4, Little Turtle—with two thousand Miami, Delaware, Pawnee, Shawnee, Wyandot, Seneca and Ottawa warriors—defeated General St. Clair's American forces at present-day Fort Recovery, Ohio.

This was the worst defeat the United States Army had ever suffered. It is probable that LeGros was with Little Turtle in this battle.

General Anthony Wayne took control of the American troops in 1792. As he traveled north, he created a series of forts. When Wayne made it to the site of St. Clair's defeat, he gathered up the remains of the nearly one thousand dead and buried them. He called the fort he built there Fort Recovery. Wayne eventually defeated Little Turtle at the Battle of Fallen Timbers on August 20, 1794. General Wayne built Fort Wayne at Kekionga, which was completed on October 22, 1794. At the signing of the Treaty of Greenville on August 3, 1795, Little Turtle and LeGros were the only Miami representatives to sign the treaty with the American government.

LeGros participated in other treaty negotiations as well, including the Treaty of St. Mary's in 1818. In this treaty, which he signed as Big Body or Metche Ketela, the Miamis were given a perpetual annuity of $15,000, a guarantee that a gristmill and sawmill would be built and a blacksmith and a gunsmith would be provided to run them and a promise that the tribe would be provided with agricultural implements.

Sometime around 1820, LeGros' power waned after the death of Little Turtle. He moved to the area at "the mouth of the Salamonie," now called Lagro. From 1823 to 1826, he received annuity payments. On April 6, 1824, Chief LeGros and other chiefs of the tribe petitioned for rails and fence lots for the Indians along the Mississinewa River.

In the 1825 annuity payment list, Chief LeGros was given $175, which was to be shared among the fifteen people living with him. There were two families, his and possibly his son's, including thirteen women and children. In October 1826, in a memorandum prepared by John Tipton, the LeGros band is listed as having eighteen members.

Charles C. Trowbridge was connected with the Indian Department in Detroit since 1820, serving as a clerk, an assistant topographer and a secretary to Lewis Cass. He interviewed the aging LeGros, possibly at present-day Lagro, during his study of the Miamis' customs and traditions in 1824–25. For his assistance, Chief Legros was given a pair of three-point blankets, twelve yards of calico, three and a half yards of cloth and one shawl, valued at thirty dollars. Cass did not care for the romantic portrayal of the Indians by such writers as Cooper, Heckewelder and du Ponceau, so he selected Trowbridge to make a serious study of Indian customs and languages. Trowbridge needed the help of an interpreter to talk with LeGros. LeGros recounted his tribe's journey from St. Joseph's River and the governmental and religious customs of his people.

In February 1825, Chief LeGros expressed a desire to visit the president in Washington, D.C., and paid for it out of his family's annuity. He was concerned about a rumor then in circulation that the president wanted to push all Indians to beyond the Mississippi. Although trips to visit the president were discouraged, LeGros was eventually given permission. On January 3, 1826, LeGros, then in Fort Wayne, left with John Tipton on his journey to Washington, D.C. At Piqua, he was given a horse to ride and later took a stagecoach. They arrived in Washington, D.C., on January 20 and stayed at the Queens Hotel. On January 27, LeGros made a speech at the War Office. On February 8, he went to see the president and, in the evening, attended Mrs. Adams's levee. He returned to Fort Wayne on February 24. Part of the return journey was by steamboat.

LeGros participated in the Treaty of the Mississinewa, signed at the Treaty Grounds in October 1826. The treaty granted him four sections of land and a house, which the government would build for him. His brick house was located in the heart of Lagro. The "public pump" on the north side of Washington Street rested on one corner of his lot. The U.S. government dug it when LeGros' house was built. The two-room house cost less than $500 and was built by Moses Scott in 1828. The brick was burned at the site for its construction. Over the four sections of land, LeGros had about ten acres of corn.

LeGros, principal speaker of the Miami Indians for many years, died on December 22, 1826, at "½ past 1 oclock." LeGros' will—dated October 30, 1826, and made just four days after the Treaty of the Mississinewa—gave all his land (2,560 acres) to John Tipton. The will was filed in Allen County, Indiana, on January 15, 1831.

The legality of the conveyance of the land remained in doubt and was the subject of charges against Tipton. In March 1834, Attorney General Butler declared that the president could give his consent and approval to validate the will. Tipton then paid LeGros' children—Chinquahquah, Wahwahsahmoi and Chingwuahquomoquah—who were named as heirs and legal representatives of LeGros, $4,000 for the land, probably to silence any complaints on the part of the Indians. For many years, there was a story in the Lagro area that LeGros' only daughter, to whom General Tipton showed marked attention, influenced him to give Tipton the land.

According to the will, LeGros was living at Lagro when he made it out. More than likely, he died in Lagro and, according to tradition, was buried between two trees on a hillside just off Lagro Creek below the Old Lagro Cemetery. John Tipton asked Hugh Hanna, later the founder of Wabash, to make a casket for LeGros. At that time, Hanna lived in Fort Wayne.

CREEKS OF WABASH COUNTY

Today, as we zip down county byways, we hardly ever think of the creeks we pass over. In the early days of the county, the waterways could not be avoided and were often obstacles to travel; wagon traffic had to find safe places to ford, sometimes going miles out of the way. However, creeks were also useful; they offered employment for settlers who used their water power to set up saw- and gristmills. Streams also provided fresh water for humans and livestock and were a way to get rid of offal. The Daugherty slaughterhouse in Wabash sat over Charley Creek so that blood and debris from slaughtered animals could fall into the creek and get swept away. Above the slaughterhouse, where the Ferry Street Ford crossed Charley Creek, honey dippers dumped their loads from the outhouses of the citizens of Wabash.

Creeks often took their names from early settlers, Native Americans, historical events and natural features. Chester Township has Pony, Ogan, Simonton, Beargrass, Swank and Clear Creeks. Ogan, Swank and Simonton Creeks were named after early settlers. Pony Creek was named for the stolen Indian ponies kept there by the Witt Gang in the early 1830s.

Lagro Township has Silver, Lagro, Enyeart, Rush, Indian, Paw Paw, Treaty, Deer, Burr, Back and Rockaway Creeks and Ross Run. Lagro was named after Miami Indian chief LeGros (an alternate spelling), who had a residence built on the banks of the creek. Enyeart and Burr Creeks and Ross Run were named for early settlers. Silver Creek was named for the stolen silver Indian annuity payment supposedly hidden in the creek bed. A ten-ounce gold nugget, along with small quantities of gold, were found in Rush Creek and the Salamonie River in this area in the 1860s and again in the 1890s.

Liberty Township has Deer, Treaty, Josina, Grant, Cart and Badger Creeks. Josina Creek was named for a Miami Indian chieftain whose village overlooked the creek and Grant Creek for an early family in the area.

Noble Township has Treaty, Burr, Charley, Mill, Kintner and Batchelor Creeks; Amber Branch; and Jackson Run. Charley Creek was named for a Miami Indian chieftain who had a village on its banks. Burr, Kintner and Jackson Creeks were named after early settlers. Mill Creek was named for the Miami Indian gristmill authorized there by the Treaty of 1818. Treaty Creek takes its name from the Treaty of 1826, which was negotiated opposite its mouth.

Paw Paw Township has Paw Paw, Bear Grass and Squirrel Creeks and Jordan Branch. Squirrel Creek was named for the Eel River Indian Niconza,

whose name meant "squirrel." Paw Paw Creek took its name from all the pawpaw trees found along its banks. The fruit of the tree is also called the "Indian Banana" and was eaten by Native Americans and early settlers. The fruit is edible when the outside turns brown and the inside becomes yellowish in appearance. In the early days, the settlers would hunt deer at night along Paw Paw Creek. They would go out in canoes and use torches to "blind" the deer. They would sink the dead deer into the creek to keep them cool and continue hunting. When the settlers were finished hunting, they collected their kills.

Pleasant Township has Squirrel, Silver, Clear and Otter Creeks. Waltz Township has Ten Mile and Mill Creeks.

EARLY MILLS IN THE COUNTY

Flour Mills

Flour mills were an early and important industry in Wabash County. Early settlers often traveled great distances to have their grain processed. Mills, therefore, became a focal point of community activity. One such mill was the gristmill built in 1845 by the Minnick brothers, Michael and John. In 1857, John Minnick sold the mill to Ferris and Lynn. Lynn allowed the old mill to go to pieces and built another mill at the site in 1871. Then, Lynn sold the mill to Martin Kesler and Samson Hoch. Early accounts state that the mill produced a superior grade of flour. This mill was the last in Wabash County located on the Salamonie.

Another mill built around the same time was the Stockdale Mill, erected on the Eel River west of Roann. Constructed in 1857, it had four floors and a subbasement with power supplied from a raceway that brought water into the mill. During the Civil War, the mill was leased to a firm to supply

Opposite, top: The Falls on Lagro Creek was an attractive and secluded spot where Lagro youth went to swim, fish and be with friends. It is located north of the Blue Star Highway, up Lagro Creek behind the cemetery. *Author's collection.*

Opposite, bottom: Paw Paw Creek was named for the pawpaw trees found on its banks. The fruit of the tree is called a pawpaw. The pawpaw, also called the "Indiana Banana," is a tropical fruit that some say tastes like a mango or melon, while others say it tastes more like a papaya. *Courtesy of Wikipedia.*

The Stockdale Mill is a prominent historical feature of Wabash County and was built by Thomas Goudy. During the Civil War, it produced ground flour for Union forces. In 2002, it was restored through community efforts led by Dwight and Susanne Fouts. *Author's collection.*

Pearson's Mill was located across the Mississinewa River from old Somerset. Starting about 1897, the mill became a recreational center with camping, fishing, boating, dancing and picnicking. A steamboat would tie up at the mill and take vacationers on a ride on the Mississinewa. *Author's collection.*

flour and meal to the Union army. A hammer mill also did animal feed grinding. Now restored, the Stockdale Mill is a fine example of early mills that supplied the needs of Wabash's early citizens.

Another mill was Pearson's Mill, located just north of the Mississinewa River across from Somerset. One of many mills on the fast-flowing

Mississinewa, in 1897 it became popular not for grinding corn but as resort area. The mill owner, a Mr. Pearson, converted the mill into a summer hotel. The old buhrs were left in place and were occasionally used to grind chop feed. The rest of the mill was divided into rooms. The entire second floor was converted into a large hall for dancing. The acreage around the mill was used for camping and picnicking, with vacationers swimming and boating in the river. The mill was swept away during a flood. Even after the demise of the mill, the area maintained a reputation as a resort for many decades. Somerset conducted many Fourth of July and Memorial Day celebrations at the resort.

Woolen Mills

Another type of mill in the county was a woolen mill. Because sheep farming was part of the county's agricultural economy, farmers needed a way to easily process their wool. There were two woolen mills in Wabash County—one at Somerset and another, the Star Woolen Mill, in Wabash. The Star Woolen Mill was erected in 1863 by A.B. Snavely and William Steele. The four-story, half-block brick building was destroyed by fire in 1893.

To process wool in a woolen mill, fleece is first taken into the sorting room. A machine with over 1,001 teeth in its cylinder, running at lightning speed, tears the wool into thousands of small pieces. It is then taken to the carding department. There, nine mammoth machines separate the dirt from the wool, dumping the former into a waste tank and twisting the latter into long, slim rolls wound around large spools. In the next room, five large spinning jacks wind the yarn around thousands of little movable wooden spikes. This yarn is taken to the warping department, where it is warped (set lengthwise to hold the tension on the loom) and made ready for the loom. The yarn then goes to the weaving department, where eighteen looms are constantly clicking away, making yards and yards of cloth. The cloth is taken to the basement, where the finished article is scoured. It is placed in a revolving kettle, known as an extractor, in which water is poured. This machinery makes more than three thousand revolutions per minute, separating the water from the cloth. The cloth is then taken to the finishing department, where it is dried, pressed and packed for shipment. This was done in the Star Woolen Mill company's storerooms, which were across canal street from the mill. In 1892, the Star Woolen Mill did $100,000 worth of business.

The woolen mill in Somerset was built by Dr. Ellis in 1865. By 1871, he had sold the two-story brick mill to William McLean and Bros. The factory had one custom card, seven looms, 240 spindles and a twister for stocking yarn. The factory could turn one thousand pounds of wool into 1,200 yards of cassimeres, jeans, flannels and thirty pairs of blankets. In August 1871, 4,500 yards of assorted fabrics produced by the mill were sent to Chicago outlets. Much of the success of the woolen mills was due to the efforts of the foreman, William Love.

HALLEY'S COMET HAS A LONG HISTORY

Halley's Comet, like all comets, comes from the frozen edge of our solar system. Every once in a while, comets come away from the edge and travel around the sun in a football-shaped orbit.

Some astronomers have described comets as "dirty snowballs" made up of ice, frozen gases, dust and chunks of rock. When one of these giant "snowballs" nears the sun, the sun's heat starts to evaporate the comet's frozen gases, causing a cloud of gas and dust to form around the nucleus. The cloud, called a "coma," together with the nucleus, forms the head of the comet. Solar winds make the gases and dust particles stream out from the head of the comet, resulting in the comet tail.

Comets give off no light of their own. What we see is sunlight reflected by the comet. A comet's brightness depends on its position relative to the Earth and sun, the size of its nucleus and the amount of matter streaming out behind it.

Some comets pass our way only once. Others come at regular intervals, like Halley's Comet, and are called periodic comets. We know from literature and other records that Halley's Comet has made at least thirty visits, dating back to 240 BC. The first known visit was recorded in an ancient Chinese silk book.

Writings on a Babylonian clay tablet told of the comet's visit in 164 BC. The famous Bayeux Tapastry, which depicts William the Conqueror's victory over King Harold in the Battle of Hastings, shows the comet. Some of its visits have coincided with major events in history, such as the destruction of Jerusalem in AD 70 and the defeat of Attila the Hun in AD 451.

People used to believe that comets were omens portending evil events or the end of the world. Miami Indians thought the world would come to an end through contact with a comet. Miami princess Kil-So-Quah once described her tribe's reaction to a comet she saw. The braves went to high ground and shot guns at it. The children ran to the old squaws, thinking the world had come to an end.

English astronomer Edmond Halley was the first to suggest that the same comet might make repeat visits. When a large, lung-tailed comet appeared in 1682, Halley tracked it across the sky. Night after night, he measured changes in the comet's position to figure out where it had come from and where it was going. Halley figured that the comet went around the sun about every seventy-six years. He predicted that it would again be visible from Earth in 1758. Although he was not alive to see it, his theory proved correct, as a German amateur astronomer saw it in December 1758.

On Halley's Comet's spectacular 1910 visit, it passed close to Earth, within fifteen million miles. That time, it was so bright that it lit up the night sky. At that time, Wabash, like the entire nation, was caught up in comet fever. There was much discussion about what evil the comet might portend. There were some who thought the world would end. However, there was no panic. Local Wabash newspapers began a comet watch in May 1910 and kept readers posed.

On May 14, citizens were treated to their first look at the comet. A long warning blast from the whistle at the Water and Light Company in Union Mills signaled its appearance. Unfortunately, this alarm came at 2:44 a.m. Citizens were roused from their slumbers, thinking that the town was burning down or, worse, that the world was ending.

After the scare died down, Wabash citizens began to scan the skies. The best place to observe the comet was from the eastern terminus of Hill and Main Streets. It was best viewed from 3:10 a.m. to 3:30 a.m. Many citizens were disappointed in what they saw, and some even confused the comet with Venus.

For the next two weeks, Wabash citizens spent their evenings riding and walking about the streets in the hope of seeing something. By May 19, a "massive ball of fire" could be observed in the western sky between 8:00 p.m. and 10:00 p.m. One farmer in Lincolnville quit working on a fence, as "its foolish to do the work now when there is no assurance that neither the fence nor I will be here after the comet comes."

The only observable effect of the comet's visit was a cold wave. In 1835, the comet's visit also caused a cold wave and snow. The editor of the *Times-Star* commented, "It never touched us! The comet has come and gone, and this old Earth is whirling along just the same as it has been whirling through the ages."

Halley's Comet won't be as bright on its next approach. The closest it ever got to Earth was about thirty-nine million miles away on April 11, 1986. Because of the glare of lights and the effects of pollution in the area around the towns of Wabash County, it was impossible to see unless one went out into the reservoirs. During January 1986, the comet appeared in the southern skies after sunset. Each evening, it appeared a little earlier and lower in the sky. Near the end of January, Halley's Comet disappeared from view as it moved behind the sun. It was out of sight until February 24, 1986, when it reappeared in the eastern sky before dawn. Morning after morning, the comet appeared brighter, earlier and higher in the predawn skies. In mid-April, the comet sank below the horizon. Halley's Comet will return in 2061. Be ready!

NEWCOMERS WELCOME AT TREATY GROUNDS

In 1826, a site opposite the mouth of Treaty Creek was picked to hold negotiations with the Miami and Potawatomi Indians. It became known as Treaty Grounds, but today's residents of the county commonly call this site Paradise Spring. One local writer said that after the Treaty of Mississinewa was signed, the cabins built by the soldiers who accompanied the treaty commissioners were left abandoned, and a decade later, Wabash rose from the site. This is far from fact. Treaty Grounds was the first white community in Wabash County, and it continued to play an active role in the area, becoming the site of many firsts in Wabash County.

Two roads had been cut to the treaty site, one from Huntington and one from Anderson. The contract to clear the Anderson road had been given to Peter Ogan, Champion Helvey and a man named Rogers in the fall of 1826. The roads were used to transport goods to the treaty negotiations. Later, early settlers found their way into Treaty Grounds on these roads. Some who came were familiar with the area, having been present at the treaty negotiations. Squatters took over the soldiers' abandoned cabins. Locally, Treaty Grounds was called the "New Comers Headquarters." Families stayed in the cabins until they found suitable land. One such squatter was Samuel McClure, the first acknowledged settler of Wabash County. Originally a trader at the treaty negotiations, he returned with his wife and ten children on January 15, 1827. The family stayed until June 10, when he built a cabin three miles west of Treaty Grounds. There Samuel and his son Samuel Jr. began a fur

In 1826, treaty negotiations were held at this location with the Miami and Pottawatomi Indians and the United States government. Today, it is the site of Paradise Spring Park. The cabins were built to house officials and traders who attended. After the treaty was signed, squatters moved in, and it became the town of Treaty Grounds. *Author's collection.*

trading post for the Ewing Company. Another son, Robert, built a log cabin at Lagro on Chief LeGros' property and moved there for a short time before moving on to Grant County. Around the same time, Joel and Champion Helvey squatted in the area until spring, when they settled at the mouth of the Salamonie River. There, they operated a ferry and a public house. In May, Benjamin Hurst—accompanied by Robert Wilson, the first blacksmith in the county—came to just "look around." Wilson found employment as the government blacksmith at Indian Mills near the Keller's Settlement and brought his family to settle there.

Another early settler who left a commercial impact was Robert Hars (also spelled Heares, Harse, Hoise and Horse). He was a "particular friend" of John Tipton's, and he was encouraged to open the first public house in Wabash County at Treaty Grounds. He used some of the cabins for his inn. Tipton thought so highly of Hars that he recommended him to run a post office at Treaty Grounds. Hars became the first postmaster of the community and in the county. The post office was established on January

9, 1828. James Foster, who was present at the annuity payment made to the Miami at Treaty Grounds, mentioned that "Mr. Hars keeps a public house" and "paid some attention to horticulture," his garden being sufficient to feed the seventy people who attended the annuity payment. The Miami evidently respected Hars, as they left his garden alone during the payment—even the "melons" he had. Hars and his wife, Mary, ran the public house until they were bought out. The Harses then moved to Logansport.

David Burr was one of the most important settlers to Treaty Grounds. He took over the Harses' public house and lived in another cabin nearby. Eventually, he became postmaster and ran the post office out of his home. William H. Coombs, the first attorney in Wabash County, stayed at Burr's Hotel, which he claimed was one of the best in all of northern Indiana.

Besides attracting settlers, Indian agent John Tipton realized the importance of the area in dealing with the Miamis. On June 4, Tipton placed a wanted ad for ten wagons to be delivered to the Treaty Grounds "by December 25th or sooner." Peter W. Banta of Jefferson County agreed to make the wagons and deliver them to Treaty Grounds. On June 28, the Kintner brothers delivered saddles, bridles and saddlebags—many of which they made at their camp at the mouth of Kintner Creek on the Wabash—for distribution as part of the treaty agreements with the Indians. Afterward, they moved to Logansport.

From June 28 to July 5, John Peter Paul, a member of a canal surveying party, stayed at Treaty Grounds while surveying the river. He kept a diary of his trip from Fort Wayne to the Tippecanoe. R.E. Banta later printed that diary in 1933 with the title *We Run the Canal Line*. On June 28, he described having a "cold bath in all its perfection" at the Treaty Grounds. He had only two complaints about the site: the rain and the fact that the "moschetos [*sic*] [were] extremely troublesome." On July 4, they "remained in camp. Mirth and music close the evening of the Fourth." This is the first known Fourth of July celebration held in Wabash County. On the fifth, they moved on to the Mississinewa River area.

During most of July, John Tipton was at Treaty Grounds making arrangements for an annuity payment. The population of Treaty Grounds swelled to over seventy people. On July 28, a payment of goods for the Miamis arrived at the Treaty Grounds, and from August 2 to 7, the goods were distributed to the twenty-four Miami chiefs present. In all, the annuity payment amounted to $26,259.47 in money and goods, including one thousand pounds of tobacco, two thousand pounds of iron, two hundred head of cattle and two hundred head of hogs. Tipton also issued orders from Treaty Grounds that a military guard was to be placed at Samuel McClure's house so that he could not sell alcohol to the Indians during the payment. Before Tipton left Treaty Grounds, he appointed Hugh Hanna to oversee the building of the Pottawatomi Mills and houses for the chiefs. Hanna was a cabinetmaker and carpenter by trade. In the official report, Tipton stated that the Treaty Grounds "has become two [*sic*] public a place" and annuity payments would have to be made elsewhere.

In 1828, Treaty Grounds continued to attract those searching for a new start. Two such men were David Patrick and Pleasant Gruble, both cabinetmakers. They walked from Fort Wayne to assess the lay of the land and look for a place to set up shop. They found Treaty Grounds, but there was no demand for their occupation, as most settlers made their own furniture. They carried on, eventually ending up in Logansport, where they became the first mechanics in Cass County.

On December 18, 1828, Cass County was formed, and what was to become Wabash County was attached to it. At about the same time, David Burr was appointed one of the first canal commissioners, and on March 21, 1829, he became postmaster of the fledgling community. On May 1, 1829, the Cass County commissioners formed Wabash Township. Treaty Grounds was made the township center. The first elections in the area were held there, and Samuel McClure was appointed election inspector. The commissioners of Cass County also appointed James Oldham as Wabash township supervisor, Champion Helvey and Samuel McClure as fence viewers, Jonathan Keller and Robert Wilson as overseers of the poor and Rodgers as supervisor of the schools (he was later replaced by Jonathan Keller and then David Burr). That fall, a mail route from Logansport to Fort Wayne was established. This was the third road into Wabash.

The Cass County commissioners also established rates for taverns, groceries and ferries in the area. The assessed fee for a license for these businesses was $7.50. Taverns run at Lagro and Treaty Grounds could charge the following rates:

Keeping a horse one night	50¢
Hay and grain	50¢
Victualing, per meal	25¢
Lodging	12.5¢
Brandy, half pint	50¢
Wines, half pint	50¢
Rum, half pint	50¢

Holland gin	50¢
Whiskey, half pint	25¢

The only ferry was at the mouth of the Salamonie River, and its charges were:

Each man	6.25¢
Man and horse	25¢
Horse, mule or ass	18.75¢
Wagon	50¢
Horned cattle over four years	6¢ each
Swine	3¢ each
Yoke of oxen	25¢
Sheep	3¢ each

The year 1830 was a busy one at Treaty Grounds. A mail route from Marion to Treaty Grounds was established, and Jonathan Keller was given the contract to carry the weekly mail between the two. The United States census was taken, and Treaty Grounds was included in the Cass County census taken by Logansport citizen N.D. Grover. If we look at the entry for David Burr, the following heads of families were recorded around him and may have been in Treaty Grounds at the time: John B. Introis, John Myers, John R. Hinton, Joseph Moreland and Jacob Hoover. There was a total of forty-three inhabitants in Treaty Grounds. After the census was completed on November 27, 1830, it was "open to inspection" at the "two most public places within the county—Logansport and Treaty Grounds as verified by Chauncey Carter at Logansport and David Burr at Treaty Grounds."

The small community had its problems. The wilderness surrounding Treaty Grounds was full of wolves, which impeded travel and settlement. The relatively new government placed a bounty of one dollar on wolf scalps in the hopes of ridding itself of the pest. It would take several more years to eliminate the pest. To the north and west of Treaty Grounds on Pony Creek, a small gang of outlaws had taken up residence. They stole horses, preyed on settlers and passed counterfeit notes.

On September 6, 1831, Grant County commissioners formed Wabash Township, with Treaty Grounds as the township seat.

In 1833, the writer of the *Indiana Gazetteer* penned the following description of Wabash:

> *Wabash, an interior county, bounded on the north by unorganized territory, on the west by Miami county, on the south by Miami and Grant, and on the east by Huntington. It extends about twenty-four miles from north to south, and sixteen miles from east to west, containing about 380 square miles, or 143,200 acres. It was organized in 1832, subsequent to the time of taking the enumeration. It is supposed the white population does not at this time exceed five hundred. The county presents a variety of soil and surface. The valleys, along the rivers, are from half a mile to three miles in width. In those valleys the forest timber consists chiefly of walnut, sugartree, cherry, poplar, ash, beech, elm, and oak, with an undergrowth of spice, plum, and hawthorn. These valleys are bounded by hills and broken lands for a distance of a mile, or a mile and a half. The table lands are either dry and rolling, or flat and wet; the soil rich and loamy, and the valleys particularly are very fertile. The flat table lands abound with willow swamps. Limestone rock is abundant in this part of the state; and it is also well supplied with never-failing springs and rivulets of pure water. The only articles of trade in this county are furs and peltry.*

The 1833 *Indiana Gazetteer* did not include any information on any community in Wabash County. It described Marion as having a store and a tavern and forty inhabitants. Miamisport (Peru) had a store, a tavern, several mechanics and fifty inhabitants. Treaty Grounds had a fluctuating population but had a post office and a public house, with probably just as many people as Marion.

On May 4, 1834, canal commissioner David Burr granted contracts for construction of the Wabash and Erie Canal west of Lagro at Treaty Grounds. The state commissioners met in Burr's home as they selected the county seat for Wabash County and again when they elected the justices of the peace for Noble and Lagro Townships. Burr's house was also used to transact the first business of the new Wabash County commissioners.

Early postmasters for Treaty Grounds were: Robert Hars, from January 9, 1828, to March 29, 1828; David Burr, started on March 31, 1829; James Sweetser, started on December 2, 1835; Abram Kensinger, started on April 1, 1837; William Steele, started on June 29, 1837; and Hugh Hanna, started on January 21, 1839. The post office was moved to Wabashtown on February 18, 1839.

In 1835, David Burr sold his Wabash interests to Hugh Hanna for "ten thousand Dollars for Town property & 400 acres of land." One of the reasons he sold was because there was talk of intersecting the Wabash and Erie Canal with another canal at Wabash, and he wished "to escape the odium of being charged with self motives." He moved to Fort Wayne and was removed from his position as canal commissioner under the suspicion of using funds inappropriately.

After the founding of Wabashtown to the west, Treaty Grounds began to lose importance, yet it continued to attract temporary residents while slowly fading away. The state continued to mail official county records to Treaty Grounds until 1839.

AN ILLUSTRATED HISTORY OF LITTLE BEAR WOMAN

In the 1930s, A.L. Duckwall made a set of postcards that tells the story of the Little Bear Woman (Maconaquah in Miami). This postcard shows the last view Frances Slocum (her English name) had of her mother when marauding Indians kidnapped her along the Susquehanna River in Wyoming Valley, Pennsylvania, in 1778. She never saw her parents again. An Indian family adopted Frances and raised her as their own; she remained with the Indians for the rest of her life. *Author's collection.*

Opposite, top: Frances was married several times but eventually married a Miami known as Deaf Man, and they settled on the banks of the Mississinewa River. Here, she is shown confiding in George W. Ewing, a trader with the Miamis, telling him her story of captivity among the Indians. Intrigued by her story, he sent a letter to Lancaster, Pennsylvania, to try to find her family. The postmaster read the letter but did not believe the story, so the letter sat in a dead letter file for several years. *Author's collection.*

Ewing's letter reached the Slocum family two years later. Two brothers and a sister made the long trip to see her. Here, they are pictured with Frances's two daughters, Ozahshinquah and Kekenokeswhwa. When Frances died, she was buried beside her house at Deaf Man's Village. In 1901, a monument was erected in her memory, and other family members and friends began to be buried there as well. The cemetery was moved to make way for a Corps of Engineers reservoir project. Slocum's remains, and others buried with her, were moved to a new location, and funds were provided for the new cemetery's upkeep. *Author's collection.*

LOG CABINS OF WABASH COUNTY

There is no more solid fixture in Wabash County and American westward expansion than the log cabin. Being born in one has been a prime political asset to office seekers from constable to president. Six American presidents were born in log cabins. Abraham Lincoln is, of course, the best known. Before him was Andrew Jackson, who was born in 1767. William Henry Harrison was not born in a log cabin but was living in a house that was half log cabin when he was elected. His campaign was the most rollicking and hilarious in all of American history. Parades and floats carrying small log cabins with latch strings and cider barrels by the door helped earn Harrison 234 electoral votes to Van Buren's 60.

One of the most disappointing things to many who visit Plymouth Rock is that the houses are not the iconic log cabin. Settlers there probably never saw a log cabin. England and the low countries of Europe had been short of timber for a long time because demand exceeded supply. The Native Americans knew nothing of lob cabins either. They had no iron and, therefore, no metal axes or saws.

Historians agree that the log cabin was introduced to America by the Swedes who first settled in Delaware around 1638, some eighteen years after the founding of Plymouth Rock. The Scandinavian countries had plenty of forests, and their people were accustomed to cabins and houses made of logs. So they built them on this side of the Atlantic too. It was not until the beginning of the eighteenth century that non-Swedes built log cabins; the Scotch Irish and German settlers in Pennsylvania were the first.

A log cabin, however crude, was a sturdy shelter. A good axeman could make a log cabin without help, except for hauling the logs to the selected site and lifting them into place. At the corners of the building, the logs were notched together like clasped fingers and held in place by their weight. Cabins were constructed using a variety of notches. Notches often varied on a single building. The most common method in Wabash County was known as the Block House End method, which was common in the Ohio River Valley. The only tools absolutely essential were an axe, a whetstone and an auger. The auger bored holes into which wooden pegs called "trunnels" were driven.

The thirty or forty trees needed to build a small cabin paid four dividends to the settler. One was the cabin itself. Another was the clearing made in the forest where the trees had been cut down. The land had to be cleared anyway for the growing of crops. Third, the pioneers needed wood to cook their food and to keep warm. The pioneer, unlike his ancestors, had access to all the wood he could burn. Lastly, the ashes from the fires could be saved and made into potash, which could be sold or made into a type of soap.

Since families usually had a large number of children in those days, cabins were generally crowded. And sometimes multiple families lived in a single cabin.

There were three basic forms of log cabins: the one-room cabin, the saddlebag and the possumtrot. The one-room cabin originated in Scandinavia and northern Germany and was the original house built in New Sweden.

The saddlebag consisted of two rooms "hung over" a single fireplace. Many saddlebags evolved from one-room cabins when another room was added. The outside recesses created by the fireplace were used to stable a few head of livestock in the winter. The possumtrot, sometimes called "dogtrot," was described as "two pens and a passage" because of the breezeway separating the rooms. The pioneers also called this breezeway itself a possumtrot. The separation of the rooms afforded privacy.

Instructions for building a log cabin are found in T.B. Helm's *History of Wabash County*, published in 1884. For a fourteen-square-foot log cabin, it was recommended to "fell a tall straight ash, maple or walnut tree." Very popular in Indiana was the yellow poplar tree, which was easy to cut down and often grew to very large size. The builder would then hew the tree "to a flat-sided shape with an adz ax." Notches were then cut down the sides fourteen feet apart. Double stakes were then set fourteen feet apart in a square on high ground. The foundation logs were placed on them.

For the roof, one had to "cut poles or small trees (six inches through), making them fourteen feet long." The ends were then scuffled to fit the notches in the logs. One end was then put in the notches, the other between the stakes. "In the notch, let the ends touch, but put blocks between the other ends, so as to give the upper one slant enough for the roof. Put some logs like the sides upon the large tree-trunk in the back wall of the house." The back of the cabin was then raised "high enough for a tall man to stand erect. Do the same across the front, leaving open space to hang a front door and frame a window."

A fireplace was a necessity and built with fieldstones. A chimney was built on the outside of the house using sticks and mud. It would later be replaced with fieldstones as well. Then one had to "build the sides up to a peak and place the roof pole" and put on the roof. Lastly, one had to chink the cracks—that is, "stuff the cracks with moss." Mud, wood chips, stubble and rocks were also used to chink cracks.

One of the earliest poems about Indiana, "The Hoosier's Nest" by John Finley (1866), included the following about log cabins:

The emigrant is soon located—
In Hoosier life initiated:
Erects a cabin in the woods,
Wherein he stows his household goods.
At first, round logs and clapboard roof,
With puncheon floor, quite carpet proof,
And paper windows, oiled and neat,
His edifice is then complete.
When four clay balls, in form of plummet,
Adorn his wooden chimney's summit.
Ensconced in this, let those who can
Find out a truly happier man.

THE TALE OF THE IRISHMAN'S POND

Early Liberty Township was much different than it is today. The forests were thick and densely filled with a great variety of wildlife, including many wolves. In fact, the beginning of the Lafontaine area lies in the community known as the Wolf Trap or the Grant Settlement. Bogs and swamps filled the area and made travel extremely difficult. In fact, the roads of eastern Liberty Township were the worst in the region. The first wagon road ran from Lagro to Connor's Mill on the Mississinewa River. Later, it was moved about a mile east to become America Road.

Elder settlers of eastern Liberty Township used to recall the story of Irishman's Pond. This was a large, swampy area made passable by means of a

Opposite, top: The Abshire log cabin is a focal point of the Roann community. Built of native timber by Alex Absure in 1863, it was donated to Roann by Jesse Abshire in 1966. It was moved to a park setting on Chippewa Pike in the middle of Roann. The site is often used for historical reenactments during the Roann Festival, which is held every September. *Author's collection.*

Opposite, bottom: A log cabin on Mill Creek Pike near Richvalley. It is located near the site of the first gristmill in Wabash County, built for the Miami Indians living on the Big Miami Reserve. The 1818 Treaty of St. Mary's provided for a miller from the government. The last miller was Jonathan Keller, who established Richvalley. *Author's collection.*

puncheon bridge; high above, state cottonwood formed an arch of branches over it. A gentle curve in this sheltered passage meant that travelers could see only a short space in front of them, so they knew of an approaching team only by the rumbling noise of the wheels on the bridge.

The area had a certain chilling feel. Lone riders passed over the dismal bridge with a sense of foreboding. Local settlers approached the bridge with dread and were often startled out of their wits by the croak of a bullfrog, the splash of a turtle or the sight of an eight-foot blacksnake coiled on the fork of a nearby bush. But above all, they dreaded meeting the Irishman's ghost.

For years, an Irish peddler roamed over that section of Liberty Township, distributing a plethora of oils and treatments for the aches and pains of the early settlers. No one knew his name, but like clockwork, he rode through the neighborhood selling his goods each month. He was an old man, and his small, stooped form and bony, broken-down horse were a pleasant diversion. On his horse, he carried two large "pill bags." Year after year, he traversed the primitive highways and always crossed over the bridge on his way north.

In the fall of 1860, this old son of Erin was noticed no more in his "regular rounds." For some time, his horse, a perfect sack of bones, wandered about

The old Irish peddler would have known this house. The Grant House in LaFontaine on Indiana State Road 15 was built in 1844 by one of the Grant brothers. The house is said to rest on logs that still have the bark on them. *Author's collection.*

the vicinity without its rider. Eventually, it was found dead. All throughout the neighborhood went up the cry, "What became of the Irish peddler?" It became an all-absorbing topic at corn huskings, quiltings and the like. His saddle and pill bags were found in an area called Christman's Woods.

Right Scott later said that at about the time the "ould Cork" (the Irishman) disappeared, he had heard a strange sound as he passed by the bridge. It sounded like a large cat screaming or a woman. He had stopped to look around and listen more intently but had never heard the sound again.

The body of the old Irishman was never found. Many believed he came to his end by foul means, possibly murder, but then, why were his possessions found? Was the sound that Scott heard a panther, so often spoken of in the Mississinewa area? We may never know. Many elder settlers claimed to hear the screams of the cat and the slow, deliberate footsteps of an unseen horse on the Irishman's Pond bridge.

Many superstitious persons still fear passing the site, though the area bears little resemblance to its former years. The trees are gone, and the bridge has been replaced by a blacktop road. Yet some claim to see the old Irishman walking along the road. Others can hear what sounds like the *clop-clop* of hooves ending with a scream.

Wabash Patriotism

On May 13, 1846, the United States declared war on Mexico, and the president asked for fifty thousand volunteers. Indiana began to raise its share of the quota. Captain Davis W. Lewis was one of the first. He headed for the small community of Wabash to raise a regiment. He spent several days recruiting in the town of about six hundred people.

War fever was high among the young men of the county. Many came to see Captain Lewis and flocked to the American flag. Before Lewis left, twelve men enlisted under his command, and another forty formed a volunteer company to train under Nathaniel Davis, awaiting a further call for troops.

The twelve who signed up were Moses W. Ross, Levi Ross, Clinton Lafavour, Abijah A. Cox, John Kizer, Thomas Hurley, Charles Rozelle, William Ebenezer, Isaac B. Rozelle, Thomas Benge and Neely Benge. The next day, the men were to leave by packet boat for Fort Wayne. That evening, however, William O. Ross, the father of Moses and Levi, confronted Captain

Lewis and demanded that his son Levi be stricken from the rolls because he was only seventeen years old. Lewis complied.

The next morning, the untried soldiers mustered and formed up near the courthouse and marched down Wabash Street to the canal landing. The men's faces beamed as they marched, and the crowd cheered them on. At the landing, many sad, tearful loved ones said goodbye. One face was missing from the crowd; Levi Ross was nowhere to be found.

Levi was not going to be thwarted in his plans to join the army and defend his country. He knew the canalboat with the troops would be going through Lagro, and he planned to meet it. He followed the towpath to just outside Lagro, where he waited by a bridge. As the canal packet passed under the bridge, he jumped aboard, with shouts of encouragement from his comrades. Off he went in defiance of his father, as many a youth would do later.

On June 22, 1846, this company of men was mustered into Company F of the First Indiana Volunteers at New Albany, Indiana. Colonel James P. Drake was the commanding officer. Of the twelve who went, three died. Levi enjoyed military life so much that when his term of enlistment was up, he reenlisted for three more years or until the end of the war. After the war, he returned to Wabash. In 1861, he again answered the call to service and rose to the rank of captain before dying in Louisville, Kentucky, on March 7, 1863.

Part II

Hidden History of Life in Wabash County

Toll Roads

Would you pay to use a road? At one time in Wabash County, you had to. If you go back to Roman times, you'll find that toll roads were common in the fourteenth and fifteenth centuries. Germanic tribes charged tolls for mountain passages. Even Greek ferrymen charged a toll to ferry dead people across the river. In the United States, toll roads began in the 1790s with the Lancaster Turnpike, which connected Philadelphia and Lancaster, Pennsylvania.

The immigrants who came into Indiana first had more or less followed Indian trails and often had to hack their way through forests. The first wagon road in this area was built in 1826; it ran from Anderson in Madison County to Treaty Grounds. The second road opened Huntington to Treaty Grounds. In order to pay for construction, it was necessary to charge a toll on the roads. Another toll road was built from Wabash to Somerset in the 1870s. It ran from the Wabash River Bridge up Columbus Street to Vernon Street and out to Mill Creek Pike, where it joined Yankee Road. A tollhouse was located there. As communities grew, the old dirt roads were not adequate, so gravel turnpike roads became necessities. In 1880, turnpikes became common.

Some of the early turnpikes in Wabash County that charged tolls were Wabash to Mount Vernon, with the toll gate south of the river on Vernon

Street; Wabash to Ashland, which terminated at Lafontaine; Wabash to Lagro; Treaty Creek to Wa-Con-nah Pike; Charley Creek Pike; Wabash and Mill Creek Pike; Roann and Chippewa Pike; Minnick Pike; Laketon Pike; Manchester Pike; A.J. Bruner Pike; Jesse D. Scott Pike; New Holland and Wabash Turnpike; and Lagro, Dora and Township Line Turnpike.

The free turnpikes were Mail Trace Turnpike; Walnut Tree Pike; Hanging Rock Turnpike; Lafontaine and Range Line Turnpike; and Dora, Huntington and County Line Turnpike.

These are the tolls listed for the Wabash and Eel River Plank Road:

One horse and rider	1¢ per mile
Additional horse	½ ¢ per mile
Score of sheep	2¢ per mile
Score of cattle	5¢ per mile
Score of horses	5¢ per mile
Score of swine	2¢ per mile
Sleigh	1½¢ per mile
Other	1½¢ per mile

During the early 1850s, plank road fever hit the West. Early successes in New York led advocates of better roads in Indiana to find out more about plank roads. Citizens of Wabash County were quick to find out about this new method of preparing roads. On January 15, 1849, the state legislature enacted the Plank Road Law. This allowed corporations to organize and build roads. By February 21, 1851, enthusiasts for plank roads within the county had formed the Eel River Plank Road Company with $6,000 in capital and sold shares for $10 each. They began to give contracts for the construction of Chippewa Pike.

Chippewa Pike started at the north end of Cass Street and ran northwesterly on the line of the Rochester Road. The first tollhouse still stands on the northeast corner of Cass and Stitt Streets. It ended at Roann, a distance of ten miles. Although it was not completed until the 1880s, it demonstrated the feasibility of such roads in opening up trade avenues into the county. The first three miles out of Wabash were laid with nine-foot-long, three-inch-thick, eight-sixteenths-inch-wide hemlock and oak planks. At the end of this section was another tollhouse located near where the Wabash Country Club was. This first section had rotted away by 1860

The tollhouse on Chippewa Pike was built in the early 1850s. It now sits at the intersection of Cass and Stitt Streets. Chippewa Pike ran from Wabash to the Chippewa Villages, present-day Rochester. The tollhouse was originally board and batten style. A toll keeper lived here and collected tolls on the improved road. *Author's collection.*

and became a muddy road. In 1882, it was completely rebuilt, covered with gravel and leveled at a cost of $3,100 per mile.

Most people appreciated improved roads, but not everyone was happy with them. Many people used the roads but got off the road before they got to the tollhouse. One night, vandals struck the tollhouse in South Wabash. They sawed the arm into three parts and pulled out the post, much to the chagrin of the gatekeeper.

RAILROAD STATIONS DOTTED THE LANDSCAPE

From the late 1850s to the 1960s, railroad stations were an exciting gateway to many Hoosier towns and cities. They were often the first contact point between the local community and the traveling public. Most were simple wooden structures that served as freight warehouses in addition to serving passenger needs. Others were very ornate, catering to every need of the traveling public. Wabash County had both.

By 1900, there were four railroad lines running through Wabash County. The Wabash Railroad was the first, traveling east and west through the county with stations at Lagro, Wabash and Richvalley. The Big Four ran north and south with stations at Rose Hill, North Manchester, Urbana, Speicherville, Wabash, Treaty and Lafontaine. The Detroit, Eel River and Illinois ran across the northern townships through Liberty Mills, North Manchester, Bolivar, Newton, Ijamsville and Roann. The C&E Railroad also ran through the northern townships of Servia, Boliver, Newton, Laketon and Disco.

The towns with a railroad saw growth; those without began to decline. Liberty Mills lost out to North Manchester, and Lagro lost out to Wabash, beginning a slow, steady decline when the Big Four bypassed them. Communities that had a railroad had access to the outside world. They could produce goods and send them off, as well as receive needed items that, at one time, were available only in larger communities. Businesses saw their orders increase, and farmers found markets for their produce. Local residents could travel on vacations and watch as their children went off to college. Men no longer marched off to war; they rode on trains. All this transpired at the railroad station.

The railroad station became a place for men to congregate and hear the latest news. Draymen lined up to carry off freight. Wagons from local hotels greeted arriving visitors. Hawkers sold their wares, fresh fruit or homemade sandwiches. Dandy traveling salesmen briskly walked downtown to find their local contacts so they could make the next train out. For a few minutes, all would be excitement and hustle and bustle. Then it was quiet and back to the same routine.

Most of the towns once served by one or more railroads now have none. Hundreds of miles of track have been torn up and the land returned to agricultural or recreational uses. The railroad stations, once vital parts of their communities, have disappeared as well. As the railroad business shifted to long hauls, the railroad stations were no longer needed, and many were demolished. In Wabash County, only one railroad station remains standing at North Manchester. It is used as the home of another business.

The city of Wabash had two stations, one for the Big Four and one for the Wabash line. The Wabash line had a simple wooden building, valued at about $100, with a huge potbelly stove to keep passengers warm. Wooden benches filled the waiting room. A telegraph office occupied one room, and there was another room for freight. At one time, there was a beer garden across the tracks where people could get a bite to eat and a "cold one" from a local brewery to quench their thirst. On the other side of the street was a house known for having thirty girls who knew how to entertain visiting dignitaries. A

The ornate Big Four (Cleveland, Cincinnati, Chicago and St. Louis Railroad) train station at Wabash and Market Street was built in the 1890s. Not only did it handle passengers and freight, but it also had a restaurant inside. The station was torn down in the 1960s. *Author's collection.*

number of candidates for president of the United States would give speeches from the back of a train at this station. The last to do so was Robert Kennedy.

Down on East Market Street was the ornate, three-story, brick Big Four station on the north edge of the train yards. The station employed about six hundred people. There was a restaurant in the eastern wing of the building. To the west of the building, one could get a free drink of sweet-tasting water from the famous Paradise Spring. About two blocks down the street, there were four hotels that catered to the traveling public.

The simple wooden railroad station at Lagro sat on the north side of the tracks and was a busy place. Surrounding it were stockyards to the west, as well as a grain elevator. A tremendous amount of farm produce went through the station. Whether travelers went north or south, there was a hotel within a block of the station—the Keller House to the north and the more popular Western House to the south. The traveling public enjoyed coming to Lagro to boat up the Wabash River to Hanging Rock. These simple railroad stations were frequent, easy targets for burglars. In 1892, the Lagro station reported that four raids had been made on its safe, with dynamite being used to blow open the safe. Each time, the burglars got away with little if anything.

The Lagro train station and Lagro Equity Exchange grain elevator on the Wabash Railroad. *Author's collection.*

Another simple $100 building was at Bolivar. Today, only four houses sit where a thriving town was once located at the intersection of two railroad lines. In 1887, E.F. Geltion moved to Bolivar to make his fortune. He was off to a good start. He set up a restaurant in the railroad station and in the month of October, he fed 356 train passengers, one of whom—Benjamin Harrison—would later be president of the United States.

Most communities found their station, whether plain or ornate, to be a source of pride. Yet not everyone was happy with their train station, and they made their feelings known. For some reason in 1888, Urbana citizens had a problem with their station. Late one night, someone dynamited the building, damaging the floor and a partition between the telegraph office and the freight room. The damage was repaired, but the station was still not up to the citizens' standards. Within two weeks, the same station was destroyed by fire while the town turned out to rejoice at its destruction. The station was rebuilt and must have finally satisfied the people of Urbana, as it was never vandalized again.

THE MAKING OF MAPLE SYRUP

The Algonquin tribes of North America, particularly in the White and Wabash River Valleys, used to refer to the full moon in February as the "Snow Moon." If you went outside after a fresh snow, you would be amazed at how bright it was. It was also called the "Hunger Moon," as the long winter could be very taxing on food resources. The North American Indians were the first to discover that "sweet water" could be boiled down to make sweet syrup. It is unknown how they first found out. Maybe someone tasted a broken branch with sap bleeding out of it? We will never know for sure.

The pioneers of this area learned the uses of "sweet water" from the Indians. February signaled the time of the year to make one of nature's treats: maple syrup. Hard maple trees (*Acer saccharum*) were "tapped" to get the sap, which was boiled down to syrup or sugar for home use or as a trade good at the local store.

From the earliest American settlement of Indiana, about 1800 to 1840, maple sugar was almost exclusively used for sweetening. The United States Census Bureau recorded that in 1860, seven million gallons were produced nationally, forty million pounds of which was sugar. In 1912, the *Wabash Plain Dealer* reported that there were "not as many sugar camps in the county any more, and every year finds more and more disappearing." It went on to say that "among the largest are those owned by William Banks near North Manchester and Dan Cooper" west of Wabash. As late as 1950, two million gallons were produced, a sixth of which was sugar.

From the sap—the sugary liquid inside a tree produced by the previous year's leaves during photosynthesis—comes the syrup. In winter, this sugar changes to starch stored in the sapwood in ray cells. When the weather warms above forty degrees Fahrenheit during the day, generally in mid-February, enzymes in the ray cells convert the starch back to sugars to "feed" the buds, which will grow into new leaves.

A daytime rise in temperature above freezing creates pressure in the sapwood, which causes the sap to "flow" out of the tree if you create a hole in the sapwood, which is called "tapping" the tree. When night temperatures drop below freezing, negative pressure in the tree causes it to recharge itself with sap from the roots. Sap travels up the tree in the xylem and down through the phloem, the food pipes. On the next forty-degree day, sap flows back to feed leaf buds and is released through the tap hole.

On trees sixteen inches or larger in diameter, tap holes should be half to three-eighths of an inch in diameter and one and a half to three inches into the sapwood. The holes should be located at waist height. Trees over twenty-four inches in diameter can support two tap holes; over thirty-two inches, three holes; and over thirty-nine inches, four holes. A spile is inserted into the tap hole to drain the sap into a bucket.

Tapping does not harm the trees, as only a small portion of sap is removed from each one. An average tap hole produces ten to twenty-five gallons of sap per season, resulting in one to two quarts of syrup. On a productive day, a tap hole may produce up to one gallon of sap per hour.

Sugar maple groves are part of stands of old hardwood forests. The best conditions for growth include an open canopy for maximized crown spread and a healthy understory to protect ground moisture and permit seedling and sapling maples. Sugar maples can grow to one hundred feet tall and have trunk diameters of twenty-four to forty-eight inches.

During the ideal harvest time, sap is clear and slightly acidic. As the season progresses, acidity increases, resulting in a darker, sometimes bitter syrup.

Once the sap is collected, it is fed into an evaporator. The syrup is almost done when the temperature hits 219.1 degrees Fahrenheit. A gallon of syrup can be heated further to create seven pounds of soft crumb sugar. Boiling the syrup 26 to 28 degrees above water's boiling point forms soft maple syrup, while boiling it 30 to 33 degrees above forms hard maple sugar.

The sap is strained several times in the process of becoming syrup, including once through a wool or Orlon filter. This catches unwanted ingredients, such as bark, bugs, debris and "sugar sand." After its final straining, syrup is heated back up to 180 degrees before bottling.

The sap is clear when it comes from the tree, but as it is heated, it changes to the amber color we are familiar with. The longer it cooks, the darker it will become. The final syrup product will be about 67 percent sugar and weigh eleven pounds per gallon. Syrup any lighter may ferment and produce mold, while heavier syrup may crystallize, causing sugar solids at the bottom of the bottle.

Natural maple syrup is healthier than imitation syrup. Tree sap contains twelve nonvolatile organic acids, six sugars, proteins, calcium, potassium, manganese, magnesium, phosphorus, iron, copper, molivian and boron. One tablespoon of natural maple syrup provides 5 percent of your daily iron requirement and has the same calcium content as an equal volume of whole milk.

Working in a sugar camp can be dangerous work. In March 1917, Mrs. Jacob Heeter, aged eighty-six, was fatally burned while at a sugar camp near her home in Chester Township. She and her daughter were boiling the sap of the sugar trees when her daughter left to take some of the finished goods to the house. When the daughter returned, she found her mother's dress engulfed in flames.

However, the process of tapping trees is making a comeback. All one has to do is drive around the countryside of Wabash County to observe a variety of buckets catching the "sweet water." The Asherwood Environmental Science Center offers tours of its facility and demonstrations the method for making maple syrup, from collection to distillation.

Superstitions in Wabash County

In the past, as well as today, people looked for ways to predict or alter the future. Wabash County is no exception. Many still believe that a rabbit's foot can bring them good luck. Most people still do not walk on a crack in the sidewalk for fear of breaking their mother's back. Some still consider white specks on their fingernails to be a sign of good luck.

Some people believe that the moon can control a person's actions or future. In the past, it was believed that seeing a full moon for the first time over the right shoulder was a good omen. If seen over the left shoulder, it was sure to bring evil events. Farmers believed that one should plant potatoes in the dark of the moon so that they would not all grow to tops.

In the early days of Wabash, it was not unusual to walk into a house or business and find a horseshoe hanging above the door. It was, and by some still is, believed that an old horseshoe kept witches away and brought good luck. The horseshoe must never hang with the open end down, or all the good luck will run out.

People also believed that dreams tended to portend the future, and if you understood them, they could keep evil things from happening. The first dream of the night was said to have especially important meaning for the dreamer.

Cats have always had a role in superstitions. People used to believe that when moving, one should not take his cat with him, as that would be unlucky. However, if the cat found its own way to the new residence, it would bring much luck. People also believed that when moving, one should not take an old broom; to do so would cause dire calamity to befall the entire family.

People carried charms, as some do today, to ward off bad luck. It was especially good luck to carry the left front foot of a rabbit killed in a graveyard. Buckeyes carried in your pocket not only kept rheumatism away but also meant you would never be without money. Carrying an onion would protect you from snakebites. If you sneezed at an early hour in the day, you would either hear some news or receive a present that very day. Mothers whose children had lost their first tooth would swallow the tooth to ensure a new growth of teeth. Putting a stocking on inside out caused things to go wrong the whole day. When women stuffed mattresses, men did not remain in the house; otherwise, the feathers would come through the ticking.

All of us have, at one time or another, heard that breaking a mirror will bring you seven years of bad luck. In earlier days, it betokened death, as did a dog scratching on the floor.

Children have also played a role in these beliefs. If a boy had his hair cut before he was one year old, his life would be cut short. If a child crawled through an open window or between the legs of tables and chairs (unless he crawled back the same way), his or her growth would be stunted. A child would grow proud if he or she looked in a mirror while less than twelve months old. Hair cut from a child's head and hidden in a hole bored in an ash tree or oak tree would prevent serious illness until he or she grew to the height of the hole. Many early woodsmen found such a talisman in a tree in this county. And finally, if a baby clung to a pencil when first presented with one, it was destined for a successful professional career.

USS *Wabash*

In its younger days, the USS *Wabash* was the pride of the American navy, the terror of many. It could circle its foe, pouring in broadside after broadside, with a nimbleness and dexterity belying its bulky build. George Dewey, who served as a midshipman aboard the ship, once said, "She was quite the finest ship of the foreign fleet and also the largest."

The steam screw frigate was laid down at the Philadelphia Navy Yard on May 16, 1854; launched on October 24, 1854; and commissioned on August 18, 1856, under the command of Captain Frederick K. Engle. Made of wood, it was 301 feet, 6 inches long and had a 51-foot, 4-inch beam; a mean draft of 23 feet; and a displacement of 1,650 tons. Its top speed was nine knots, about ten miles per hour. It had the honor of carrying President Franklin Pierce, served as Hiram Paulding's flagship and was part of the expedition that stopped the William Walker filibuster expedition. From 1855 to 1859, it cruised as flagship of the home and the Mediterranean squadron commanded by Commodore Elie A.F. LaVallete.

On May 16, 1861, it was recommissioned and was the flagship of the Atlantic Blockading Squadron. It was also flagship of the first combined amphibious assault of the Civil War, securing Hatteras Inlet and taking Forts Hatteras and Clark. In the bombardment of the forts, the USS *Wabash* distinguished itself. It was one of a fleet that rained shells on the Confederate fort at the rate of twenty to twenty-eight per minute and at last compelled the unconditional surrender of the stronghold, with 645 prisoners. The Confederates had only 4 killed and about 25 wounded, although the fighting lasted nearly two days, and the Federals had none killed and none of their ships damaged.

The USS *Wabash* was the hero of the Battle of Port Royal on November 7, 1861. It was the flagship of over seventy-seven vessels and sixteen thousand army troops. The seventh dawned bright and clear, with scarcely a ripple disturbing the waters of the bay. Fort Walker, which guarded the channel with its sister fort, Fort Beauregard, opened fire with heavy guns. The USS *Wabash* answered with its bow guns, and then, when within full range, it opened its formidable broadsides.

Dismayed, the Confederate vessels fled up a creek into the sound. As flagship of Flag Officer Samuel Francis Dupont, the *Wabash* led the Federal fleet. This steam frigate, with its two ten-inch-, twenty-eight nine-inch-, fourteen eight-inch- and two twelve-pound guns, was a brave sight. Its men crouched, eager for battle, and Commander Christopher R.P. Rodgers watched through his glass for the moment when the command to fire would be given again.

The *Wabash* turned down Hampton Roads, its enfilading fire wreaking havoc on Fort Walker. At last, it was fairly abreast of the fort and not more than eight hundred yards distant. Being the flagship, the *Wabash* received the largest share of the enemy's attention. One shell passed between Captain Dupont and Captain Rodgers, narrowly missing each of them. Past Fort Beauregard, the *Wabash* led the fleet, and then it turned and, for the second time, bore down on Fort Walker—this time within three hundred yards. The air was filled with smoke, sand from the shore and the flash of bursting shells.

Again the *Wabash* turned and passed the fort, opening its broadsides as it slowly drifted along, and at last, when the forts were silent, the *Wabash* ran close to the batteries and fired one gun. There was no reply. A boat with a flag of truce put off from the *Wabash*. Some minutes after, its crew entered the fort. Captain Rodgers was seen scrambling up the highest part of the ramparts, carrying the stars and stripes. At the first glimpse of the ensign, the suspense gave way, and thunderous cheers came from every craft in the fleet.

The fight had lasted for over three hours. The Federal loss was eight killed and twenty-three wounded; the Confederates had eleven killed, four missing and forty-eight wounded.

The *Wabash* took part in the expedition against Fernandina in February 1862; was flagship of the Atlantic Blockading Squadron until 1863, under Rear Admirals Dupont and Dahlgsren; and was active in the blockade

The USS *Wabash* AOR5, a replenishment oiler, was 659 feet long and had a 96-foot beam and a 36-foot draft. The U.S. Navy names oilers and gasoline tankers after Indian words for rivers. *Author's collection.*

of Charleston, South Carolina. It took part in the bombardment of Fort Fisher in North Carolina from 1864 to 1865, then commanded by Captain Melanethon Smith. The USS *Wabash* was classy; even at the end of the Civil War, a sailor described it as a "bright white interior marked by the glass black guns and carriages." The USS *Wabash* had four men during the Civil War who won the Medal of Honor.

From 1866 to 1871, it was laid up for repairs at Boston, and for two years, it was the flagship of Rear Admiral James Alden of the Mediterranean squadron.

The *Wabash* was decommissioned on April 25, 1874, at the Boston Navy Yard. From 1876 to 1912, it served as a receiving ship in the Boston Navy Yard. In the fall of 1912, the Navy Department decided to sell it. It was sold as scrap on November 15, 1912, to the Boston Iron and Metal Company. It was burned to make it easier to get to the metal out of it. Five of its ten-inch Dahlgren smoothbore cannons were transferred to the National Civil War Naval Museum in Columbus, Georgia, in 2010.

Pictured underway replenishing a guided missile frigate, the USS *Wabash* AOR5 had a top speed of twenty knots. Its armament was four three-inch guns. It carried a complement of 369 men and officers. It was scrapped in 2013. *Courtesy of Wikipedia.*

Of all the activities aboard the USS *Wabash*, eating chow in the mess was the most favored. Out of all branches of the military service, navy men and women are known to be the best fed. While at sea, the cooks, butchers, bakers (commissary rating) and stewards served three meals a day to the crew of 369. *Author's collection.*

Three more ships carried the *Wabash* name. At the beginning of World War I, the German cargo ship the *Tubingen* was impounded by the United States. Later, it was turned over to the United States Navy and was commissioned on February 1918 as the USS *Wabash* ID1824. It carried cargo to France until April 1919. It was decommissioned on April 21, 1919, and eventually ended up in the Italian fleet.

The third *Wabash* was a Patapsco-class gasoline tanker AOG4. It was laid down on June 30, 1942, at Seattle, Washington, and launched on October 28, 1942. It was commissioned on May 10, 1943, and assigned in the Pacific Theater to Service Squadron 8 and later 10. It supported operations at Iwo Jima and Okinawa. After World War II, it was decommissioned on July 29, 1946, but reinstated on June 1, 1950, for the Korean Conflict. It had a mixed American and Japanese crew and was deactivated on September 10, 1957. It was eventually scrapped.

The last ship to be called the *Wabash* was a replenishment oiler of the Wichita class AOR5 (1971–94). It was laid down on January 21, 1970, by

General Dynamics Quincy Shipbuilding in Quincy, Massachusetts. It was launched on February 6, 1971, and commissioned at the Boston Naval Yard on November 20, 1971. It served in Western Pacific operations during the Vietnam War and was decommissioned on September 30, 1994, and scrapped in 2014.

The French Family Murders

On Saturday night, October 7, 1854, a whole family was murdered in Wabash County, about five miles west of Wabash in the Richvalley area.

Aaron French, his wife and five children lived in a small cabin on the James Lewis farm. Early in the fall, Aaron French had been ill and unable to work. In September 1854, John Hubbard and his wife, Sarah, were boarding in the French home. On Saturday evening, several neighbors visited Aaron French, who was still sick. The Hubbards were still living with the family. The next day, Sunday, James Lewis and others stopped to inquire about Aaron's health. Before they reached the house, the Hubbards informed them that French and his family had gone away to Iowa to live with his brother. The visitors asked John what had become of the property French owned. He said he paid French forty dollars in gold for all the personal property located in the house.

The sudden disappearance of the French family caused a lot of talk. The Hubbards' conflicting statements aroused suspicion. The subject of French's departure remained a mystery until December 1854. Edward Boyle, a canal worker, was missing. He had boarded for a while with the Hubbards. As a canal laborer, he earned about $500. When, on March 23, 1855, the water was drained below the canal lock opposite the Hubbard cabin, a man's body was found. A coroner's jury determined that the man had died from a blow to the head and stab wounds. The body was buried.

Developments of the coroner's inquest seemed to point to John as the murderer, and he was arrested on March 27, 1855. Four days after the examination, there was a preliminary hearing before Justice of the Peace Esquire James. John was committed for trial on a charge of murder in the next term of the Wabash Circuit Court. On March 26, the body of the murdered man was exhumed and identified as Edward Boyle, who had been missing from the Richvalley area since the early part of winter. Before Boyle disappeared, John had had no money. After Boyle went missing, people noticed that John suddenly had money. There were other indications of John's guilt.

Hubbard's arrest for the Boyle murder resulted in Sarah's arrest as an accessory to the French murders, as stated later in the trial. The clue to the murder was obtained accidentally. After the arrest and imprisonment of John Hubbard, Sarah was allowed to visit her husband in jail. John asked her how the family under the floor was doing, and their conversation was overhead. Sarah Hubbard was arrested on Sunday, April 6.

On April 8, Constable Miles Morgan went to Richvalley and talked with Isaac Keller, who lived near the Hubbards. They decided to search the Hubbard residence. They removed some of the floorboards. Fresh dirt was heaped up on one place. They pushed a cane down into the loose earth; the cane touched something, causing it to bounce. Inserting a pickaxe and passing it through the loose earth brought to the surface the body of a child about fifteen months old. Morgan and Keller started a systematic excavation. While this was going on, a coroner's jury of six men was assembled. The bodies of seven persons were exhumed; Aaron French, his wife and five children were buried in one grave. The father and mother were at the bottom, then the eldest child and the others, according to their age. The infant was on top, next to the surface. Each skull had been broken with a hammer. Mrs. French's neck and one leg were broken. She was almost nude except for her underwear, and the others were dressed in their ordinary clothing.

On August 2, 1855, the grand jury indicted John and Sarah Hubbard for the murder of Aaron French. In court, they chose to be tried separately. John Hubbard was arraigned on the murder charge, pleading not guilty. A trial held in Wabash found Hubbard guilty, and he was hanged. Sarah Hubbard was tried in Marion, Indiana, found guilty and sentenced to life in the women's prison in Indianapolis.

Belden

Elijah Hackleman laid out Belden on May 13, 1856, for its original proprietor, Archibald M. Kennedy. The town consisted of thirty-four lots sitting next to the Wabash River and Erie Canal and the nearly completed railroad. The plat was recorded on June 2, 1856. Its north–south street was Main Street, and its east–west streets were First and Second Streets. Early owners of lots were Howard Nixon and Co., J.C. and William Raymond,

William L. Ross, James Anderson, Matthew Lynn, John G. Dyer, Christian King Philip King, W.D. and Henry Ross, Henry Ordendahl, John C. Bechtold and Koehler, Fahl and Frankenfield.

It was said that the village got its name from a man named Belden who built the first railroad bridge—a high, wooden covered trestle—near that location. The wooden bridge was replaced in the summer of 1884 by an iron bridge. The bridge was re-decked in 1898. It had five 150-foot spans for a total of 750 feet. It was 23 feet high. In 1910, the Indiana Railroad Commission ordered it to be replaced. In all of its history, there was never a wreck or an injury on this bridge. One reason was that the railroad hired two men as bridge watchers, one on either side. Men who had this job were John Dyer, William Taylor, A.C. North and James Wilhelm.

The only addition to Belden was Matthew Lynn's addition of fifteen lots between the railroad and the millrace, which was recorded on February 5, 1878. The north–south street was Mill Street, and the east–west streets were Wabash, Lynn and Franklin Streets. Early purchasers of lots were Daniel Speicher, Aaron C. North, F.R. Ferris and Thomas B. Kerr (who later sold to Elizabeth Culver). All that remains of Belden today is a grocery store (now a residence), traces of the milldam and five houses. Where farmland now exists was once a sawmill, a gristmill, a blacksmith, a grain house, a schoolhouse and a few dwellings.

The sawmill built by Jack Ross was later owned by Matthew Lynn, whose son George managed it until starting a grocery. In 1884, Adam Fisher took over the mill. John Hull ran another sawmill in town but moved it just north of Lagro in 1878.

Matthew Lynn built the gristmill in 1869. It had three runs of buhrs and was the only mill propelled by the Wabash River in Lagro Township. It was called the Belden Flouring Mill. By 1878, Lynn was shipping out four carloads of wheat over the Wabash Railway. In March 1881, Lynn sold thirty-two thousand pounds of flour alone. James M. Deck moved to the Belden area around 1880 and learned the miller's trade. In 1883, he and his family moved to Roann, where he was the owner and manager of the Stockdale Mill for over thirty-four years. In 1884, Lynn changed the flouring mill into a full roller process. He purchased the necessary machinery from Case Manufacturing Company of Columbus, Ohio, at a cost of $2,000. Lynn employed six millwrights in the mill after putting in the new equipment. The new capacity of the mill was fifty to sixty barrels of flour per day.

The milldam also provided a good supply of ice in the winter for local people to gather up a supply. There was also good fishing at the dam.

Numerous fishing parties from as far as Andrews and Pleasant View would come and spend the weekend camped on the banks of the Wabash. It was noted in local newspapers that "they reported a good time, and lots of fish." Below the milldam, close to the mill, was a favorite community swimming spot.

Samuel James ran a general store in Belden until 1877, when George H. Lynn purchased it. In 1881, N.L. Morrison purchased a 50 percent interest in the store, and it was known as Lynn and Morrison. Lynn also had a huckster wagon that he used to travel around the countryside exchanging goods in. One stop was always at the farm of John Schmalzried, who made pure maple sugar from the trees on his property and always got a good price for it. In 1878, Lynn also ran the post office out of his store. It was a gathering place for many of the locals. One Saturday, it was reported that twenty-three men and boys were in the store at one time. Lynn had a very playful pup that the men and boys liked to tease. They would spit tobacco juice in its eyes, tie strings to its tail and just pester it in general. Lynn and Morrison sold the store in October 1884 to try their luck in Kansas.

This is the Lynn and Morrison General Store in Belden, now a residence. Built before 1877, it not only provided goods for the community but also ran a huckster wagon around the surrounding countryside. *Author's collection.*

In March 1878, Belden became a station on the Wabash Railway. George Lynn was appointed ticket agent by the Wabash Railway Company. A siding had been put in, and the train went through six times a day. People from the surrounding area would get on the train at the Belden station to go into Wabash or Huntington for the day. It was said at the time that "nearly every train leaves or takes passengers." One Saturday morning, two ladies were "seen running to get on the train going west. But the railway trains run faster…and they failed to make connection. Ladies, we know this was unpleasant and we advise you to be on hand a little before train time hereafter." In 1885, the Wabash Railway Company took up the switch at Belden because of the great inconvenience to the farmers of the area and Lynn's mill. More and more of the grain trade went to Lagro.

The village continued to grow, and in the spring of 1878, Robert Hiers, from Peru, purchased a lot from Matthew Lynn and put up a building for a shoe shop.

Various diseases spread through early communities, and Belden was no exception. There were bouts with typhoid fever, lung fever, pneumonia (in winter and spring), diptheria, catarrhal fever, scarlet fever, measles and mumps, along with broken bones of all sorts. In May 1879, a doctor settled in Belden. Dr. S.M. Clark was "late of Philadelphia" and a graduate of the Jefferson Medical College. A week later, it was reported that "the Doctor is gone and Belden is desolate." Drs. Renner, Hale and Biggerstaff traveled from Lagro to meet the medical needs of the community.

The only way for early settlers to get across the river to Belden was a ford across the river just below the dam. Another ford, Kelly's Ford, was located about a mile west of Belden. In the 1880s, a bridge was constructed across the river at Belden. The bridge still remains but has been improved over the years.

There were three schools within a mile of Belden. Early teachers were a Mr. Owens, George Stephens, Alexander Fulton, Anderson Martin, Sarah Owens, Luella Rhamy and Stella Adams. In 1878, when the Risser School was ready to close for the year, the teacher, Anderson Martin, and students gave an exhibition. The exhibition opened with the song "My Old Cabin Home," sung by by William Shanghrue, followed by a declamation by Ida Fullhart, which "was delivered nicely." Belle Miller, Ebba Badger, Maud Bowers and Stilman Fullhart also presented declamations; Abner Risser even gave one in German. Then came the dialogues, followed by singing. There was a double quartette presentation, and Lew Munger sang "The Old Kentucky Shore." The program was extremely well received by the

The main attraction in Belden was the flour mill. It was the only flour mill on the Wabash River in the county. The river was easy to ford in this place, and after the dam was constructed across the river, it was even more fordable. The county built a bridge, which is still standing, as shown in this picture. Over the years, it has been widened and redone. Also in the picture is the millrace that carried the water from the dam to the mill. Now it is only a ditch, but at one time it provided power, and the young men of the community could swim in it. *Author's collection.*

community, and the only problem was the stage giving way about halfway through the program.

Not to be outdone, the Swamp School, whose teacher was George Stephens, conducted similar exercises. Oftentimes, schools closed with a carry-in dinner for the patrons.

Schoolhouses not only educated the young but also were centers of the cultural life of the community. Political rallies, churches, Sunday schools, weddings, parties of all sorts and traveling shows were held at the schoolhouse. One year, a group of eleven tramps camped in the schoolhouse until they were run out.

The Methodists of the area used the schoolhouse for preaching and Sunday school. The Lynn, Hushaw, McClure, Fox and Ferris families attended this church. Although membership was small, the church had a large and popular Sunday school. Sunday school attracted as many as fifty people. In 1878, a fundraiser was held at which eighty people were in attendance having a good time and presenting two homemade quilts made by the ladies of the town. The first baptism at this church was in May 1878, when four people were taken in a procession to the Wabash River and baptized. They did not have a full-time pastor, so ministers from Lagro and Antioch filled the pulpit, including Reverend J.A. Lewellen and Reverend Mott.

In 1881, Reverend C.H. Bella started a Sunday school at the Rock Hill schoolhouse. Reverends J.M. Pickard, Lambert, J. Bartmas and H. Rupley conducted services there as well.

For fun, Belden residents attended ice cream parties, dances, birthday parties and weddings. Weddings were an exciting time for the community. The old custom of a shivery was common in Belden. One night, the community was awakened "from our slumbers by the firing of pistols and midnight howls which caused us to repair to the window to determine the noise at that hour. As we sat there we could distinctly hear strains of beautiful music such as could be produced by none other than the cow bell pealing forth upon the midnight air." The honored couple was Frank Hood and Fanny Dunham.

Not all was peaceful in Belden. Occasionally, there was a runaway buggy, rocks thrown through a window, petty theft, fights or a confrontation in the streets. There was a family who lived two miles away from Belden, and every time they came to town, they fought with each other in the street, ending with the husband whipping his wife home. In 1879, Mollie Ross began to fuss at her brother about some reports "about him that were both dirty and true." He seized her arm and proceeded to severely hit her with his fists. A cousin would not interfere, as it was "not his fight." In 1884, a house of ill fame, located just northwest of Belden, was in full swing. Townspeople sent the house notice that it would be treated to a "storm of rocks and clubs, and probably ten pounds of hell powder, unless the inmates flee from the wrath to come."

J.L. Slagle walked away from his family. He left home saying he was going to Andrews but ended up in Nebraska before returning home. The cause of his departure was domestic trouble.

There were petty thefts in the community—corncribs were broken into and chickens, meat, butter, potatoes and even soap from a window were stolen. J.C. Bechtold had eighteen pounds of chicken feathers stolen from an outhouse. When J.W. Weaver laid a fresh supply of pork in his smokehouse, he took to sleeping in there with a shotgun to keep out marauders. It was printed in local newspapers that the petty thief should "wait til the snow disappears...and change his shoes before appearing" in public.

Caroline Waterbeck, a servant in the household of Fred Grossman, disappeared one morning. She had gathered up all her possessions and left during the night. No one knew where she went or why. It was a source of concern to the whole neighborhood. Seven months later, she gave birth to a son and sent a messenger to inform William Grossman of the fact. He planned to flee, but his father offered him four dollars cash, a new suit of clothes and a silver watch to remain.

In 1880, Belden had a population of about forty. There were seven different families: the Lynns, the Kings, the Hildebrands, the Dyers, the Taylors, the Mirchers and the Tolings.

In March 1884, John Holdy bought the old warehouse built by Archibald Kennedy and converted it into a cheese factory. In June, Holdy disappeared. He had gone to Ohio, picked out a bride and brought her back with him. In August, Holdy got into a fight with Newt Murray, and "several well directed blows were struck before they could be separated." What caused the problem was never reported, but in October, Holdy and his wife left for parts unknown. It was later learned that he was indebted to Murray for $1,000. Thus ended the brief life of the cheese factory of Belden.

During the presidential election of 1884, it was claimed that there was only one Democrat in town; everyone else was Republican and would vote for Blaine and Logan. Joseph Mackey and J.T. Hutchens came to town and spoke at the schoolhouse on the benefits of a Republican administration.

Slowly but surely, the community lost its importance to Lagro and Andrews. Belden retained the post office until 1897. Today, it just a quiet intersection on the Wabash River passed by time. All that remains is the Belden Bridge, the old general store and, one mile west, the Belden Cemetery.

THE SECOND WORST CRIME IN WABASH COUNTY

From the March 31, 1859 issue of the *Wabash Weekly Intelligencer* comes this account of what was considered the worst murder committed in Wabash County:

About a year ago, William Joy was arrested and confined in our jail on a peace warrant, sworn out by his wife. The preliminary examination took place before Justice McGuire, who required him to give bail. Not being able to do this, he was confined to prison until the next court was in session. On the hearing of his case, Judge Matlock required him to give bail for his good behavior for sixteen months. This he could not do so remained in jail. At the next term of court, Maria Joy, his wife, and Nancy Joy, his daughter, appeared before the grand jury, and upon their testimony, an indictment was found against him, which charged him with the murder of his infant son, John Joy, sometime in the fall of 1857, by holding it, naked, over the fire until it was so badly burned that it died a few days afterward. Until now, little was known about this.

On the first day of the next term, Joy was brought into court and plead[ed] *"not guilty." The court assigned him counselors: Messrs. Pettit and Cowgill and Hon. J.D. Conner, and a day fixed for his trial. A defect in court session occurred, so the grand jury was recalled again. At this time Joy was tried again and found guilty of manslaughter, and sentenced to the penitentiary for eighteen years.*

This case created much excitement, more than the Hubbard case had in the past. The principal witness in the case was Nancy Joy, the daughter of the defendant. It was her testimony that convicted William. Her mother's testimony was ruled out. It was the simple, truthful, childlike story that condemned her father for eighteen years. Her story was this:

Her little brother John, a child about four months old, was quite unwell, and had been so for some days, and was fretful, and had cried considerable during the night and disturbed her father. Early in the morning, her father called to her and told her to get up and make a fire. She did so—made the fire of brush and after the fire began to burn, the child continuing to cry, her father became enraged, and snatched the child from its mother's arms, tore every article of clothing off it, and took it by one arm and one leg, and held it over the fire until it was burned in several places to a blister. He then struck the child two blows with his hand, leaving upon its body the marks of his fingers and then threw it into a cradle.

William's wife and daughter had tried to get the child away from him when they realized what he was doing. Maria ran into the house so she wouldn't hear the screaming when William took down his gun and pointed it at her. He then left the house and did not return for several days. William told his wife and daughter that if they ever said a word about the incident, then he would kill them, so they keep the secret until after William was committed to jail for another crime.

THE RING OF THE ESCAPED SLAVE

At one time, Wabash County was part of the famed Underground Railroad. Prior to the Civil War, slaves escaping from the South would follow the Drinking Gourd north to Canada. One line of the Underground Railroad ran from Jalapa to Lafontaine to Hicksite (Lincolnville) to Lagro to New Madison (Servia) and on northward. In the 1850s, one slave was caught in Wabash County.

He was placed in the county jail to await the arrival of his owner. The owner sent a slave hunter to pick him up. The slave hunter bragged of his expertise in capturing runaways. He had captured over $150,000 worth. The sheriff reluctantly turned the slave over to him. They left Wabash on a canalboat heading down the canal. On board the canalboat were several men who were partial to the abolitionist movement. The slave had been shackled by the feet and hands, and then the shackles were fixed to a big ring around the slave's waist. He was chained to the boat when they began the trip. Several men kept the hunter below deck playing cards while two others tried to free the slave. They were able to get the chain fastened to the boat free but not the shackles. As the canalboat was passing through Richvalley, the slave jumped to the bank with the shackles on and began to run. The slave hunter, hearing a disturbance, went above deck to see what was going on and saw the slave running for the woods. He also jumped off the canalboat and went after him. Eventually, he shot and killed the slave, leaving his body where it lay. Several of the men who had attempted to set him free left the boat and found the body. They took the shackles and chains off and buried the slave where he was found. The chains and shackles were taken back to the jail in Wabash.

The sheriff's office kept the chains and shackles for years. It would occasionally use links in the chains for whatever purpose it might devise. The large link in the middle, however, was bolted to the floor and used to tie difficult prisoners to the floor until the new jail was built in 1880. At that time, the chain ring was the only thing left of the pre–Civil War days in the county. It was given to the clerk's office, where it remained a novelty for years. Unfortunately, sometime before 1930, the heavy, metal, three-inch ring disappeared. Some thought it was given to the museum. It may someday turn up in the museum or in an old, forgotten drawer in the clerk's office.

A GLIMPSE OF LIFE IN WABASH COUNTY IN 1867

Occasionally, we think about how nice it would be to go back to the good ol' days, when the pace of life was slower and more enjoyable. But was it really so good? By using the diary of Newton Fowler, who was living in 1867, we can catch a glimpse of early life in Wabash County. Fowler moved to Wabash County in the early 1830s with his parents. Newton had a farm located just to the west of US-24 and Indiana 13.

As a farmer, he spent most of his time planting and reaping crops; tending and feeding his livestock; and repairing fences, machinery, his barn and his house. Day after day, there was always more to do. Being a man, though, he could easily escape the drudgery of family and chores with a trip into town or to the mill, which he often did. In town or at the mill, he caught up on the local goings on. His diary gives us a capsule view of life in those faraway good ol' days.

All aspects of life came under his purview. He recorded those who had been married and those who had died. Nearly 150 people died that year, from many different causes—getting run over by a sleigh (many sleigh accidents were on Canal and Wabash Streets, where people would speed and show off), irresipelus, old age, lung fever, strangulation, getting kicked by a horse, carriage accidents, getting run over by trains and so on. The eldest person to pass away was eighty, and the youngest was an infant abandoned in an outhouse by its mother.

Accidents occasionally happened, such as Christian Harter getting run over by his own sleigh. Joel Brewer was getting a load of gravel at Wiley Wilson's between Wabash and Lagro when the embankment gave way, crushing his wagon to pieces. Joel survived. Mary Burget was horribly burned by an exploding can of coal oil when she tried to fill a burning lamp. Her sister saved her by throwing water on her.

Wind and snowstorms endangered life and limb as well as property. On January 25, twelve inches of snow fell, stopping even the railroads. The ice buildup on the buildings in the towns endangered the lives of passersby.

The Wabash County Poor Farm began to provide for the needy of the county in 1853. In 1867, it was called the County Infirmary, as it housed not only the poor but also the aged and sick residents of the county. *Author's collection.*

The weight of the snow and ice caused John Christman's grocery shed to collapse, scaring people and horses. Later in the year, a team of horses left under a tree in the town of America was killed when high winds blew the tree down onto them.

The town of Wabash had grown from roughly 1,400 inhabitants in 1860 to 4,000 in 1867. The county likewise was growing, but the population was already shifting from country to town life. With the growth of the towns came another set of problems for the citizens to deal with. In Lagro, the people passed their thirty-ninth ordinance, which fined anyone who hitched his or her horse to a public pump one to three dollars. In June, Derrick Lehmer petitioned the county commissioners to incorporate Somerset. It was decided to leave the decision up to the citizens of Somerset.

So many buildings were going up in Wabash that they were having a difficult time keeping track of them. The city council wanted to number the doors of businesses and houses, but the Hebrews of the city would have no part of this.

The county commissioners had problems appointing constables, upkeep at the poor farm, with the county jail, with roads and, most disconcerting, with granting liquor licenses.

Business was the lifeblood of the county, and it was expanding. T.F. Payne built a new wareroom on Miami Street. At one time, the Daugherty and Steele packinghouse had over three thousand hogs in pens awaiting slaughter. Hanna's Corner underwent repairs, and a new sidewalk was installed. The Busick brothers' two-story store at 35 Canal Street was built. The storeroom was 154 by 23 feet. On Wabash and Main Streets, just south of the courthouse, Lewark's butcher shop opened.

As some moved in, others moved out. The *Wabash Times* did not have enough business and closed up. —— Wharton closed his photographic studio and moved to Rochester. —— Schlegelmilch sold his boot and shoe store to Hoover, Bruner and Company and moved on. Major Kidd left the *Plain Dealer* and went into the army; he was stationed in the West.

The Wabash and Erie Canal, as well as trains, brought goods, services and people through the county. Wabash had its inventors. Richard Johnson applied for a patent for a timber and drying apparatus. French and Vandegrift received one for a car coupling devise. Three turnpike companies were organized to reach out to other communities such as Lincolnville, New Holland, Lagro, Dora and Mount Etna.

The county had its saints and its sinners. Churches were growing and expanding to suit the needs of their members. Methodists, Baptists and Presbyterians began or finished new buildings. The Christian church on Hill and Miami Streets was finished, and Bishop Luers dedicated the Catholic church on West Maple Street. Revivals lasting up to two weeks were coursing their way through the county. The Methodist Church of Paw Paw saw thirty-eight people converted due to the preaching of Reverend Shackleford.

The various churches took a stand against temperance and gambling. Churchwomen held socials to raise money to pay for their church endeavors. A young men's chapel that held up to ninety people was built. Donation parties were held to raise money for veterans and their families. Wabash raised $350 and Somerset $200 for those in need.

Church people who meant to uplift the community quickly found an element that did not want their help. Pettit and grand juries were set up to deal with the crime that came with growth and progress. There were affrays. The most serious was between John Morgan and George Stark. Stark struck Morgan with a spade several times. Both were fined. Joseph Miller was arrested for house burning. There were counterfeiters at Lagro and thieves of all sorts throughout the county. Someone broke into Dr. Bender's store in Laketon and stole $300. The thief then went to Lautzenhiser's store and made a meal of sardines and oysters. Most disturbing was the discovery of the body of a baby in E.S. Ross's privy, which was placed there when the infant was still alive. The Court of Common Pleas had over 127 cases to deal with that year.

The social life of the community centered on the churches, but the young men who had returned from the Civil War wanted more. They felt Wabash should have something for everyone. They organized Post 1 of the Grand Army of the Republic, the Wabash Zouaves and the Mystic Tie and attempted to bring in the YMCA and baseball.

Cary Cowgill organized the Zig Zags, the first baseball club formed in Wabash. They met and practiced at the Whiteside's Woolen Mill and a vacant field south of the canal. The Zig Zags were beaten in their first game against Peru. However, they won their second game against the Perseverance Ball Club of Huntington.

In winter, there was skating, sledding and sleigh riding to occupy Wabash's citizens. If you did not own a sleigh, you could rent one for one dollar. Both Union and McKibbin's Halls brought in cultural entertainment such as the Bohemian Bell Ringers and Franklin's Celebrated Negro Minstrels, and the local Wabash Silver Band performed as well.

Twice a year, a circus would come to town to lighten pocketbooks with its shows. People had to be wary of the pickpockets who worked the crowd. The big circus this year was the Robinson's Grand Combination Circus and Menagerie with ten shows for fifty cents.

The Wabash County Medical Society had over eleven members and regularly met to discuss cases such as tubercular and cerebrospinal meningitis and held a clinic on a little girl suffering from disease of the hip joint.

The Agricultural Society planned for the county fair, including what premiums to pay to the winners. The 1867 fair featured the American Giant Colonel Orr from Ohio, who stood seven feet, ten inches tall and weighed a massive 653 pounds.

As in just about every other year of a presidential election, the Republicans and Democrats organized their respective groups to raise their parties' pole and then fought to keep the pole standing, to slug it out at the polls with fists as well as a few slugs of another sort (drink).

Schools also came under the scrutiny of the community. Singing schools were very popular for entertainment and meeting people. The Union High School was up and running—the walls were whitewashed, floors were scrubbed, there were new blackboards and six teachers had been hired. Emma Harter taught vocal and instrumental music. The Female Academy at South Wabash was active, and the German population was clambering for, and got, a German school. The Indiana State Teachers Association met at New Albany, and Wabash canceled school so that local teachers could attend.

Around the county there were other events that kept Wabash County people talking. There was the discovery of a mastodon skeleton in Waltz Township. Hank Carmon's lively cat killed twenty-seven mice in one hour. There was the horse show at Marion where Hugh McKahan won a whopping twenty-five dollars. The state legislature was meddling again. It had passed an act forbidding the trapping, snaring or shooting of all things quail. There was the death of Black Jim (age forty), the oldest horse in Indiana, owned by Colonel Hanna. Bonnets and needle-gun skirts were the latest whim in ladies' fashions. Still want to go back to the good ol' days?

THE AFRICAN AMERICAN METHODIST CHURCH IN WABASH

The history of the African American community is hidden deep in the shrouded mists of the history of Wabash County. African Americans were a part of the county's history even before its settlement. A number of years ago, the skeleton of a black man who lived on the Meshingomesia Reservation was discovered along the banks of the Mississinewa.

The 1840 United States census shows three black families: the Gordons, the Henrys and the Tiduses. They all lived within the county even though they were not permitted to do so by the Constitution of Indiana. By 1850, a black registry kept by the Wabash County clerk listed twelve men.

By 1869, there was such a large African American community that they began to seek ways to join together socially. One of the first things they did was meet at the home of Joe Davis. Davis, with four others, organized St. John's African Methodist Church. J.H. Hill was appointed temporary pastor, and the first services were held in members' homes. Later, services were held in the old courthouse. As the church began to grow, it found other places to meet, such as empty rooms in the courthouse, a rented storefront at 27 West Canal Street and then the old Baptist church on the southwest corner of Hill and Cass Streets.

The charter members were Daniel Brown, Mary Alexander, Mary Cummings, Lonnie Brown, Janet Brown, Ada Seabolt, O.G. Brown, Mary J. Russell, Mamie Russell, Octavia Daniels, Minnie Ferguson, Katie Daniels, S.R. Waldron, Mary Harris, Maggie Black, Theodore Jordan, Julia Jordan, Thomas Johnson, Florida Johnson, W.H. Russell, James E. Johnson, Jane Waldron, Viola Johnson and Ella Johnson.

In the early 1870s, the church's members began to plan a permanent home for their congregation. Dan Ferguson and Joe Roberts located a site at 174 East Sinclair, and a frame building was erected in 1876. The lot cost $250. To help pay for and maintain the church, the members formed a Jubilee Choir and performed concerts throughout the county. They also conducted the very first cakewalk in Wabash in 1886 to raise money. A.W. Hill of the Diamond Paper Mill gave the church an organ in 1892. The frame church was used until 1903, when a stone church was erected at the same site. This church served until it was torn down in 1972.

Membership had risen from the initial five to thirty-five by 1884. By 1921, there were forty-two members. Then began a steady decline until only twelve members were on the rolls in 1961.

Preachers who have served the church are J.I. Hill and Madison Patterson, 1869; A.J. Knight, 1877; Robert McDaniel, 1880; Hezekiah Harper, 1887; Nixon M. Jordan, 1890; Reverends Hart and Colvin, 1892; Everett Gregory, 1893; J.I. Hill, 1893–94; William Collins, 1894; followed by William H. Kane, James Alexander, B.F. Coleman, F. Williams, J.W. Saunders; Reverend Boston, J.H. Hartford, S.P. Byrd, W.B. Baber, B.W. Roberts, W.H. Pearson and James E. Lyons, 1903 (exact years unkwown); U.S. Harrison, 1921; and Polk W. Wall, 1923.

THE HISTORY OF FALLS CEMETERY

Falls Cemetery is the final resting place for over twelve thousand people. It is made up of three different cemeteries: Hanna Cemetery (Old City Cemetery), originally located on East Hill Street; the Independent Order of Odd Fellows Cemetery, adjacent to Falls Cemetery; and Falls Cemetery (New or Charley Falls Cemetery).

The Wabash Cemetery Society, organized on February 6, 1862, established Falls Cemetery that same year when it purchased outlot thirty-two, northeast of Charley Falls. It originally consisted of twenty acres, six of which were used for the sexton's house, which sat between Stitt Street and Charley Creek. Robert Hall was the last sexton to live in the house, which was torn down in the 1990s. The remaining fourteen acres extended from Falls Avenue on the northwest to the bottom of the hill on the east, about fifty yards behind the present toolshed. The first burial was two-year-old Francis Rettig on August 1, 1862.

An interesting feature of the original plat was a space fifty- by seventy-five-feet that was reserved and named "Chapel Park." A bandstand was built on the spot, and on patriotic occasions such as Memorial Day or the Fourth of July, the Wabash City Band would play concerts from the stand. Often, Wabash residents would pack picnic baskets and have their dinners while listening to the music. Today, what is left of a ring of giant cedars commemorates the spot. Another usual spot was the Soldiers Memorial Park, where Memorial Day services were held. A square that is now unused once had four mounted cannons, gunstocks and a flagpole to honor Civil War veterans. All around the square, prominent soldiers of that war are buried.

In 1894, John W. Snyder, the sexton, placed the following in the local newspaper: "Parties have been interring still-born infants in Falls Cemetery without notifying me of the fact. They are running a great risk by so doing, as the law will be enforced if it is not stopped." Another problem was the cemetery found itself running out of space for additional burials. Since its opening, the cemetery had made 1,646 interments. To alleviate the problem, the society purchased an additional twenty-seven acres along Falls Avenue extending northwestward to the present fence and then running over to Colerain Street.

During the 1930s, the cemetery faced the same problem. The society purchased an additional forty-six acres following Colerain east to Cass Street. This acquisition made the total area of the cemetery ninety-three acres.

Rich, poor and those who are little known or not known at all lie buried in Falls Cemetery. One small stone carried the following inscription: "Unknown man found dead at Rich Valley, July 22, 1946." Not far away is a red stone with a lion engraved on it, marking the resting place of circus performer Terrell Jacobs, the "Lion King."

Falls Cemetery is the resting place of former mayors, congressmen, judges, saints and sinners. One stone some five feet tall marks the grave of Jennie Wade. Wade left her estate to fund scholarships for Wabash County youth

There are unusual gravestones in Falls Cemetery. This is an example of one incorporating many different emblems that show the interests of the Shambaugh family. Another gravestone was cut in the shape of a pile of newspapers because the deceased was the editor of the local newspaper. Other gravestones have traditional carvings of clasping hands, lambs, pointing fingers and lodge emblems. *Author's collection.*

Many of the twelve-thousand-plus burials in Falls Cemetery are soldiers who fought in wars of the United States, starting with the War of 1812. Pictured here is the grave of Flight Officer James R. Schetzsle of the Army Air Corps. He became a bombardier on a B-29 crew made up of nine men. Eight of the men died on a training mission over rural Kentucky on July 1, 1945. *Author's collection.*

who wanted to further their education. Another forgotten benefactor is T.F. Vaughn, president of the Wabash Cabinet Company, who built the softball field behind the Women's Clubhouse.

It has been estimated that there are over one thousand veterans, from the War of 1812 to the Lebanon Crisis, buried in Falls Cemetery.

The grave of Wabash co-founder Hugh Hanna. Originally buried in the Old City Cemetery, his remains were moved to Falls Cemetery in 1907. Besides co-founding Wabash with David Burr, he served as the first Wabash County treasurer and also served as county agent. He was responsible for Wabash becoming the county seat and built the first courthouse and jail. *Author's collection.*

Over five hundred have military memorials dedicated to them. The highest-ranking military man buried there was General John B. Rose, who served in the War of 1812, receiving honorable mention for his role at the Battle of Plattsburg. One other individual, Macy Overly, was the first soldier from Wabash County to die in World War I. Bill Gray was a navy seaman stationed at Pearl Harbor when it was bombed by the Japanese. He retired from the navy years later as a lieutenant commander.

Hanna Cemetery was the second cemetery to be incorporated into Falls Cemetery. It was the first cemetery in Wabash, established by Hugh Hanna in 1836. By 1900, Hanna Cemetery had nearly five hundred burials, including five veterans of the War of 1812 and twenty from the Civil War. The cemetery fell into a sad state of disrepair. In 1907, Mayor Joseph W. Murphy secured the deed and the right to remove the bodies. Nearly 90 percent of the exhumed bodies were removed to Falls Cemetery. Most were buried in a row behind the black section, but many, including Hugh Hanna and William Steele, can be found scattered throughout the cemetery. The original cemetery became Hanna Park.

The Independent Order of Odd Fellows (IOOF) Cemetery makes another part of the cemetery. At one time, a great number of Wabash citizens belonged to this fraternal organization. They began their own cemetery in a small area north of the toolshed. It was laid out and owned by the local IOOF lodge. For many years, it was unkempt, and many people wondered why it was so neglected. When Rose Zimmerman died around 1949, she left the bulk of her estate to the IOOF lodge in Wabash for the care of the cemetery. Unfortunately, the lodge had long since disbanded. The judge of the Wabash Circuit Court asked the board of directors if it would accept the bequest and care for the little cemetery. The board agreed, and some $12,000 was turned over to it.

In 1971, the Wabash Cemetery Society Board set up a trust fund that continues the maintenance and upkeep of the cemetery. Income is also derived from the sale of lots, grants and bequests to the cemetery. In the 1990s, the board of directors erected a columbarium to house the ashes of the departed. This was erected just off Colerain Street. In 2009, a new building was constructed in the sunken gardens section. The building includes a chapel, two offices and a kitchen. The chapel has seating for about one hundred people and is available for small funerals and interment services during inclement weather.

WINTER FUN

Wintertime in Wabash County was not as dull and dreary as we may sometimes think. Life did not slow down; people went on with work, chores, visiting, going to town and going to school. When snowdrifts formed on the rail fences on the north–south roads and snow blanketed the earth, sleighs of all shapes, sizes and conditions became the main form of transportation. Many were fancy, with intricately carved artwork and long, curved runners, while others were of a much older breed, with stout runners, rude seats and a large, flat bed. Popular kinds of sleighs were embraces, cutters, bobsleds, lizards and jumpers. "Jumpers" were the most common; being the most primitive, they were also the easiest to make. All one needed were two slender hickory poles, a few wooden pegs and an old store box.

Some of these contraptions were used to haul goods. One Wabash man even devised one to haul goods on the frozen canal bed. Other sleighs took kids to school. Nora E. Porter Stoops grew up in the Hopewell area. During the winter, she would walk in the tracks of the sleighs or, more likely, climb the drifts and roll down the other side.

Nora knew how to dress when riding in the sleigh. Her shoes were well-oiled, tanned leather. Her underclothes were heavy cotton flannel, while her woolen drawers were made with bands that would button below the knees to her knitted stockings. A heavy coat covered her wool clothing. She wore a breakfast shawl low over her forehead, folded under at the sides, brought across her nose and mouth and then tied behind her head.

Sleighs were also used for pleasure. Young men wrapped in jean clothing and furs taken from varmints, which they had killed and skinned themselves, were often seen in the evening. Sitting up straight and holding the reins with one hand, they showed off their prowess to the young ladies. If the men were good, they would be invited in to visit. There were many activities in the evening for young people, and sleighs got them there. There were literary societies, debates on all manner of topics, spelling bees, oyster suppers, taffy pulls, singsong parties and dances to attend.

Young men were judged by their ability to handle a sleigh. A young man who could handle a horse and sleigh with one hand while holding his fair companion with the other would have his pick of young ladies. One young man in the Treaty Grounds area was having difficulty mastering this skill. One day, he filled his father's empty barn with snow, hooked up the sled to the family horse and practiced his technique. His father thought he was "daft" when he caught him doing this. He asked his son, "What in tarnation are you doin'?" The son replied, "Practicing for Saturday night."

Many a young couple used the sleigh on those cold nights for courting. A considerate young man would have a buffalo robe, as well as a foot warmer, to cover his companion. This foot warmer was a slab of limestone heated in the fireplace and put on the floor of the sled. Occasionally, sleighs could be seen near a cabin, and the couple was either "sparking" or "spooning." You could always tell a "spooner"; he used one hand for the reins.

South Side Streetcars Had Their Problems

In 1891, South Wabash was annexed to the city of Wabash. And by 1901, streetcar tracks were laid through the South Side. These tracks started at the Wabash Street Bridge and extended all the way to Boyd Park.

According to a story by Dorwin Pearson, Ed Unger drove the first round trip from Boyd Park to Wabash. When a break occurred in the cable under the car, lengthy delays and repairs were necessary. On an early morning trip, as the car came through the South Side, people in their long nightshirts ran out to see the new car.

Sometimes when a local stop was made for repairs, ornery young boys would pull the trolley from the overhead cable, shutting off the power. The motorman would then get out to replace the trolley. On one occasion, this gave the boys time to soap the tracks up the slight grade that was just ahead of the car. When the car reached the soaped area, the wheels spun and the car gradually rolled backward down the hill. Finally, with a long, fast start, the car cleared the soaped area and continued on to make up time. Escapades like this weren't that unusual, even at the turn of the century. The tracks on Columbus Street were always a favorite target of South Side boys.

According to Cecilia Mills, girls could involve themselves in streetcar antics too. Girls used to put pins on the tracks in the form of an *x*. After the streetcar ran over them, the girls would have a little pair of scissors.

One of the drivers lived on Pike Street at the end of the tracks. When he finished his runs each night, he would take the pole down and leave the car on the tracks. One night, several boys at a very late hour hooked up the pole and went for a joy ride to Vernon Street. They went to Ray's Station, where they hooked up for a run to Marion. They were home before the conductor was up, and he was none the wiser.

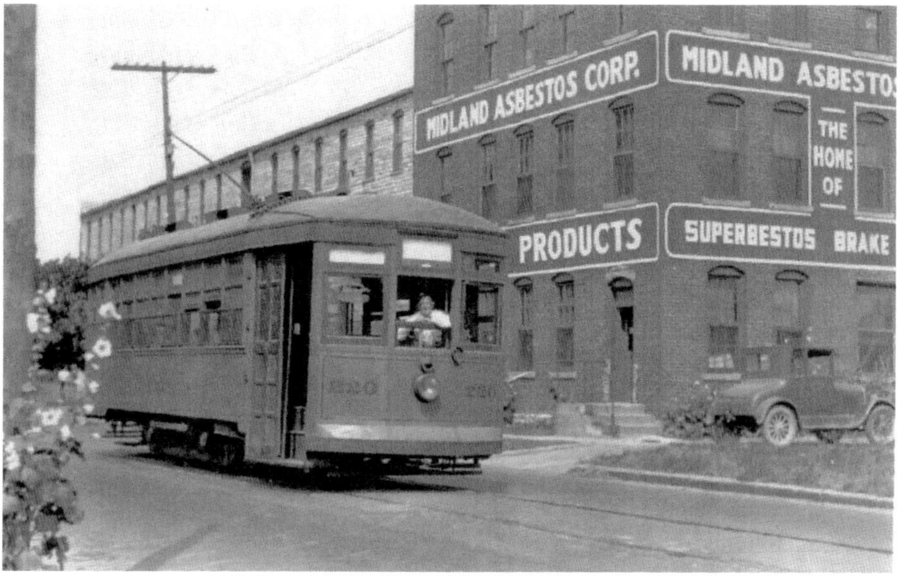

The Wabash Electric Street Railway Company was formed in June 1894. Wabash streetcars ran from what is now Ford Meter Box on Manchester Avenue to the end of Pike Street on the South Side. Another loop ran down Market Street around the business district and back to the main line. When the car reached the end of the line, the conductor would move the line connecting to the electrical line and take a seat at the opposite end. *Author's collection.*

Two Wabash streetcars pass on South Wabash Street. Columbus Street always posed a problem for them. They would have to speed up on South Wabash to make it up the hill. Sometimes, South Wabash youth would soap the tracks and have a laugh at the expense of the conductor and passengers. When the streetcar hit a patch of soaped track, it would slide back down the hill. *Author's collection.*

According to Darwin Pearson, when there were funerals at the Quaker Cemetery on Mill Creek Pike, whole carloads of people would charter a streetcar to the cemetery and back. And in 1913, the earth caved in under the streetcar at the intersection of Vernon and Columbus Streets.

Even with its problems, the South Side streetcar affected the lives of most citizens in one way or another.

Part III

Hidden Entertainment

Gypsies Will Gladly Tell Your Fortune

From the 1890s to the 1930s, bands of gypsies camped in Wabash and spread throughout the town, eager to tell fortunes and relieve citizens of whatever coins they had.

According to a 1901 issue of the *Plain Dealer*, droves of gypsies camped by the river. And in another newspaper in 1928, two carloads of gypsies swooped down on Wabash and quickly went to work to get what money they could out of people by telling fortunes. They worked fast before the police officers corralled them and sent them on their way.

Women—with their full skirts, gaudy kerchiefs and rings in their ears and noses—went into business telling girls their fortunes. They would say, "Come, pretty girl, you will have good luck. Put a nickel in your hand, hold it there, and I will tell your fortune. Good luck, and you'll be married to a tall, dark man—or, make the coin larger and no woman will stand between you and this man." Then a quarter was used by the subject, finally a half dollar or maybe more—whatever the girl was willing to pay. The gypsy then passed on to the next girl. The gypsy could pick up a good deal of money in record time by telling more or less the same story.

Chief Bolte and the sheriff soon started them on their way out of town; however, they landed at Lagro and began the same business of fortunetelling. In Lagro, one filling station man, when approached by the gypsy wanting to tell his future, said, "All right, in just a second." He then put his watch and all his change into his pocket, buttoned up his vest and coat, offered his hand and said, "Let's go." But the gypsy was not so eager to tell his fortune with no "loot" to expect.

In yet another Wabash gypsy story, this one from 1912, a band of gypsies in three wagons hit town, supposedly from Ohio. The group was composed of eighteen, including children, and said they were from South America and their language was Greek. It didn't take them long to scatter over the town, and as it was September, they were eager to work fast and get to warmer places.

From the reminiscences of Hazel E. Bridges Miller comes this story:

> *The gypsies were real, however, they traveled with several horse-drawn wagons loaded with everything imaginable. Some of the wagons were covered and dark eyed children and their elders would often be seen peeping out from them. They usually had some mangy dogs and an extra horse or two tied on behind. They would want to tell your fortune in exchange for a chicken or a duck and if you were not at home, they often got a fowl without any palm reading.*

Parents often frightened their children by telling them to stay away from gypsies, as the gypsies would carry them off and they would "never see their family again."

A story told to the Wabash County historian about his house was interesting, to say the least. A gypsy fortuneteller lived near General Tire and often told people's fortunes. One day, a brand-new Oldsmobile went missing on Ferry Street. The wife of the car's owner went to tell the gypsy and asked what had happened to it. The gypsy told her exactly where it was. The husband didn't believe in such "foolishness" and told his wife so in front of the gypsy. A day later, the car was found right where the gypsy said it would be.

The gypsy walked to the house on the northwest corner of Thorne and Ferry and, from the sidewalk, put a curse on the house and family. Shortly afterward, the family would hear coal running from one end of the basement to the other. It was so disturbing that the family moved out within a month.

The same historian related another first-person account about a band of gypsies in the late 1970s at a spot west of Richvalley. The gypsies were traveling in four vans, painted in all different colors, instead of wagons to travel across the country. Each one was loaded with dozens of people.

Outsiders are called *godjo* while the gypsies are the "Roma." There are approximately twelve million gypsies around the world today. Generally, they are dark and swarthy in appearance. The Roma can be traced back to Asia and were found in Persia by AD 1000. A nomadic group, they spread into Europe and were in Paris by the 1400s. They had their own brand of religion, which included a great deal of mysticism. Fortunetelling was primarily done by women, as they believed they had a gene in their system to tell fortunes. Being nomadic, they did not stay in one place long, and as a result, their formal education was limited.

Gypsies first came to Virginia in 1801 or 1803. The separate groups did not compete with one another. Most women were married by age of thirteen, and to avoid trouble with the law, they had two birth certificates—one for their real age and one for legal purposes.

THE MISINFORMED TEACHER

One fall day, as a group of boys was walking to school near Slabtown in Noble Township, they spied an unusual object in a nearby tree. Upon investigation, they found a hornet's nest the size of a bushel basket attached to a tree limb. From then on, every time they passed that hornet's nest they had a longing to possess it. Finally, one day at recess, the older boys hatched a plan for smoking out the hornets and removing the nest. They thought it would look good hanging in their classroom. They discussed their plans with their teacher. The teacher ruled against the plan, as the hornets were still very active, and suggested they wait until the hornets all died off.

One student asked, "How will we know when they're dead?" The all-knowing teacher replied, "I'm told there's always a sentinel on guard at the entrance of the nest. When that guard disappears, you will know that the hornets have died, as only the queen lives through the winter."

The days passed unbearably slowly for the boys. Every day they passed by, and one of the boys would check the mouth of the nest to see if a hornet guard was there. One morning in late October after three hard frosts, the boys reported that there was no guard at the nest. They all agreed that the nest would come down at noon.

All the boys and girls of the school turned out to witness the expedition. Just across the road from the tree with the hornet's nest, there had once been an old sawmill. All that remained was a twenty-foot iron smokestack and some other old junk. The smokestack, which was lying on the ground, was about two feet in diameter. All the girls and younger students found seats on the smokestack to watch the older boys remove the hornet's nest.

One of the older boys was named Ken. With much showmanship and catering to the crowd, he climbed the tree and slowly worked his way out on the limb. His weight helped him bend the limb down so that Mike and John could catch the tip of the smaller branch to which the nest was fastened and remove it. And then all bedlam broke loose.

The hornets weren't dead after all! In fact, they were alive and *mad.* With their nest jerking and bobbing up and down, one can imagine them stirring from sleep and muttering to one another, "What's going on here?" Out they came by the hundreds.

Ken, the nearest person to the nest, was in a precarious position, and they went for him. He quickly slid off the limb and tried to swing himself down the tree. But he lost his hold and came crashing to the ground on all fours. Without rising, he dove headfirst into heavy weeds and bushes,

A group of students at the Treaty Grounds school sometime in the 1890s. Students generally went to school from 6:00 a.m. to 6:00 p.m. They were given one hour for lunch and devised their own ways of having fun. Games such as red rover, steal the bacon, hide-and-seek and ball games of all sorts were indulged in. If a creek was nearby, it offered many opportunities for exploration. If a hornet's nest was nearby, it could lead to serious problems. *Author's collection.*

swatting every which way at the little devils. Another swarm of hornets went for Mike and John and anybody else in sight. Most of those sitting on the stack just fell backward off it and then rose and ran screaming, their arms flailing.

Mike had on a big wool hat that flapped around his ears as he fled followed by a battalion of winged beasts. Several of the larger boys dove into the smokestack for cover, one after another. Those behind shouted frantically to those in front to move up, complaining as they were kicked in their faces. John, flapping his arms and zigzagging, finally headed for the smokestack. By that time, it was nearly full. He got his head and shoulders inside, so the hornets attacked him in the rear. His howls of pain were punctuated by angry commands to the others in the pipe, "Git outa here! You fellers got no business in here! Why don't you move up?" About this time, a hornet got into the hair of one of the older girls, and her shrieks and wild gestures added to the pandemonium.

In a comparatively safe position a few yards away, the teacher laughed at the funniest spectacle he had ever seen. Ken looked at the teacher out of his one good eye, the other being swollen shut, and said, "The story about the sentinel at the entrance sounds kinda fishy to me!" The teacher replied, "It does to me, too, now. I must have been misinformed."

BOYD PARK

Boyd Park years ago was a place, so they say,
Where action was reigning and night life would sway.
The old interurban of trolly and track,
Would bring people out and then take them back.
I heard about this when I was a lad,
The tales of enjoyment the young people had.
—Raymond Thompson

Boyd Park was named after Frederick Coleman Boyd, who had organized a company to set up an interurban line. The park was created in 1900 to generate revenue for the interurban system. Ron Thrush said, "Actually what they did, they built a streetcar line, starting out at Ford Meter Box, right straight through Wabash, going across the Wabash Street Bridge, through South Side and out Mill Creek Pike, Cooper Road and across the bridge to

Boyd Park." Clarence Pulley remembered "boarding an open-sided streetcar in downtown Wabash loaded with people hanging on both sides of the car." The streetcar line was closed in 1904, when a Cleveland syndicate took over and consolidated the line with the Fort Wayne Southern Traction Company, which was located on the north side of the river.

The streetcar and interurban were not the only ways to get there. A paddle-wheel boat called the *Launch Togo* also carried people to and from the park. At one time, there was a dam at the bridge to keep the water high enough for the boat. That was "a unique thing to see a paddle-wheel boat going up the Wabash River."

Boyd Park was a source of family fun for people from miles around, beginning its first full season in 1902. The park featured a theater, a hotel, restaurants, boating, entertainment, amusement rides, games and possibly the first roller coaster in Indiana. Originally called a "Scenic Railway," it was a huge wooden structure winding its path through the park. The park covered eighteen acres south of Richvalley, along the north side of the Wabash River. Area residents were treated to various vaudeville acts, musicals, balloon ascensions and well-known entertainers. The park housed a pavilion, as well as a stage and dance hall. There was a "terrific amount of activity down there" during its heyday. In 1902, nine hundred people attended the grand opening of the Boyd Theater. Howard Powers and Dolly Theobald, the favorites of the evening, performed *The Runaways*, a one-act comedy. They were followed by Tom Browne, who did some original work as a whistler; the Thompson sisters, vocalists and dancers; the Esterbrooks, comedians; and finally the kintegraph (moving pictures). After the show, a large number of the patrons remained for the dance that followed in the pavilion.

The rest of the 1902 season featured such acts as comedians John D. Gilbert and George Yoeman; the Esther Wallace Company, which performed "Love Finds a Way" and "My Wife's Presents"; the Garrison Sisters, Manning and DuCrow (monopods); the monkey circus of Professor Tony Ryder; the Musical Kleists; Musical Thor; Newel and Niblo playing novelty instruments; Signor Macceo and his talking dog; Frank and Ida Williams, who performed in the controversial blackface; and "Whistling" Alfred Holt, among many others. The Fourth of July celebration was the highlight of the season. Ballgames were held at 10:30 a.m. and 3:30 p.m.; the theater put on three performances; there was dancing at the pavilion in the afternoon; and the early evening was illuminated by fireworks. Nearly eight thousand people were at the park that day. It took until 4:15 a.m. to get everyone home from the park.

In 1906, Fred Fowler, a vocalist from Wabash, was drawing large crowds to Boyd Park. Fowler would sing popular songs while hand-colored photographs on glass slides were projected on a screen, a performance style called a "magic lantern show." When Fowler finished, the words of the song were written on slides shown on the screen by a magic lantern, and the audience was encouraged to sing along.

During the summer, the park featured weekly specialty programs. In June, the Beggar Prince Opera Company performed four comic opera plays—*The Beggar Prince*, *Girofle-Grifla*, *Olivete* and *Fra Diasolo*. Each show cost twenty cents. Beginning on June 14, there was a weeklong skating program that ended with a dance. The dance cost twenty-five cents for men and was free for ladies. June 17 featured Sipe's Dog and Pony Show, with Sherman and Fuller, comedy acrobats; Wilson and Wilson, magicians; and Ms. Duryville, who created shadowgraphs. July 16 featured high-class vaudeville acts, including the Melroy Trio, singers and dancers; Misses Delmore and Reily, cornet soloits and duettists; Ed Maussery, comedian; and Mime and Fern Clerise, who sang along with illustrations. The Innes Great Band, Restorff's thirty-piece New York Metropolitian Band and Kryl and his forty-two-piece band performed at the park as well. Near the end of the season there was a Wild West show featuring fifty people—cowboys, cowgirls and Mexicans—and thirty horses. Twice during the year, there were special balloon ascensions.

The 1908 season began on May 29 and featured Garguilo and his Italian band. J.A. Irwin was the manager of the park and promised good shows because the "economy was such that entertainment troupes were looking for work." Shows cost fifteen cents each, and matinees and evening shows cost twenty cents each. The type of shows that were included were *A Trip to Indiana* by the Herald Square Opera Company, *A Jolly Widow* by the Harley and Burns Company and *New England Folks* and *The Stanton's Curse* by the Barton Stock Company. Quartets had become popular, and the following were on the programs: the Tocadero Quartet, the Cowboy Quartet, the Brothers Devan and a military quartet. High-class vaudeville acts were also on the program, including Billy Link's Musical Comedy and Vaudeville Company and Major Mueller's Vaudeville and Musical Comedy Company. The programs were well attended, but crowds were starting to go the Friendship Home at Lukens Lake, and Pearson's Mill was gaining in popularity for those wanting to go picnicking.

The highlight of the year, as always, was the Fourth of July, which featured Billy Link's Musical Comedy and Vaudeville Company, a fireworks display and a band that went into Wabash to serenade and then returned to the park to play during the day. A new feature for the park was a baseball team called the Boyd Parkers. They invited local teams to play against them and, for a time, had an enviable record. The team was made up of —— Elshire, —— Manning, —— Fisher, O. Elshire, C. Downey, R. Gant, O. Downey, L. Garner and C. Crist. In July, J. Levering Jones, president of the Wabash Valley Interurban Company, toured Boyd Park, and shortly thereafter, an article appeared that suggested that either Boyd Park or Robinson Park in Fort Wayne would be closed because of a lack of attendance.

Early in the 1908 season, J.A. Irwin, who had been in charge of the park since its opening, began looking to rid himself of the park. He told the *Wabash Plain Dealer* that "my lease for Boyd Park is expired and next season I will conduct an open air theater in Peru." He went further, saying it was the intent of the owners to "establish a country club, with golf links" at the park.

In December 1908, Irwin faced ten indictments for operating the park on Sunday in violation of the Sunday "blue laws." Ten charges were also filed against Joe Small, who ran the roller coaster. It was announced that the owners would close the park, but during the winter, Joe Small struck a deal to lease the park for the coming summer.

In May 1909, the manager, Joe Small, announced the season was off with a "boom." Small had help from W.J. Beardsley, Albert Nichter, W.J. Clayton and Nick Kindler. The roller coaster and concessions were on full blast, with new pieces of furniture placed around the park for the comfort of the visitors. Throughout the season there were free dances, concerts and baseball games. The park received more competition from Lukens Lake but also Matter Park in Marion, Pearson's Mill and the Wabash City Park. To tone down its image somewhat, Boyd Park began to advertise that it was "a place to hold Sunday School picnics and reunions." The park added boating and fishing to things that could be done at the park. Also competing for patrons were the Eagles Theater and the new Dreamland Theater.

The programs offered at the park were not as frequent as in the past. Giuseppe Creatore, an Italian bandmaster, was so popular that the interurban line put extra cars on its train to accommodate people from as far away as Fort Wayne and Toledo. Other bands that performed were the Shaff Brothers Band, Henderson's Schoolboy and Girls Musical Comedy Band, the Third Regiment Band and the Fraser Highlanders Concert Band from Toronto, Canada. Besides sensational vaudeville acts, there were balloon ascensions, acrobats, the Osborne Dog and Monkey Show and Crotty, the "Prince of Blackface." Plays, as always, were popular, and the season's fair included *Divorce Question*; *Thirty Days in the Shade*; *Jim, the Westerner*; *The Sunny Side of Broadway*, performed by Max Blom and the Dancing Pippins; *The Millionaire Kid*; and *The Girl from U.S.A.*, featuring the American Beauty Chorus (entrance fees were doubled for this one!).

The 1910 season began with a promise that Boyd Park would be presenting "tabloid musical shows of an elaborate style" on Sundays. The park opened with *Happy Land*, performed by the Empire Musical Comedy Company. The park advertised less in the local papers than it had in previous years, taking advantage of articles submitted rather than space purchased. On May 28, District 11 of the Federated Clubs held a picnic convention at the park, sponsored by the Wabash Round Table. Dinner was served at the inn for those in attendance. Still, the year was off to a slow start.

All of the main holidays—Memorial Day, Fourth of July and Labor Day—were celebrated in a low-key manner reflecting prevailing society values. Free shows, especially fireworks, and dancing, the usual fare, were gone. In June, the interurban cars lost power as park attendees were ready to return home. People were given a choice of walking five miles into Wabash or staying the night at the inn. Many chose to walk home. On July 3, the crowd was so sparse that when a show was postponed due to rain, it was not put on when the rain stopped.

A review of the shows reflects the park's decline. Shows included *The Wall Street Detective*, *Divorcons*, *A Brother's Revenge*, the Goffney Musical Comedy Company and *The Yankee Doodle Boy*. The company that put on *The Wall Street Detective* was at Boyd Park for five weeks. Fewer bands were scheduled to appear at the park, but those that did perform included the Elks Band of Logansport, the Electric Technique Band and the Mudtown Minstrels. Fewer acts performed, and often they were not even named on the program bill.

When spring rolled around in 1911, Pearson's Mill opened in May with a candy stand and all its boats overhauled, repainted and given a formal cleaning. Lukens Lake, now called Friendship Home Park, opened in mid-June with the Chili band performing and a large crowd in attendance, but there was no Boyd Park. Prevailing Sunday blue laws had taken their toll. The roller coaster was taken to Triers Park on the west side of Fort Wayne. Boyd Park lived on only in the collective memory of county residents.

DAREDEVILS "ENTERTAIN" WABASH CITIZENS

Early downtown business leaders came up with a way to bring business downtown: they would provide entertainment for the vast crowds that would descend on the downtown area. As early as 1871, the businesses hired a daredevil to perform for the crowds. Professor LaHoune was a monopod (one-legged) tightrope act, walking across a rope that stretched across Canal Street and performing his tightrope act hourly. The crowd was amazed at his feat; word spread, and crowds got larger each night. As the businesses had hoped, the spectators spent more money.

From then on, Wabash had its share of daredevils—persons who tried to defy the elements of height, space or logic. What makes a person try to act in a dangerous way? Just to entertain? Or for money? What makes us want to watch them? It is hard to know the answers to those questions, but the daredevils still show up, and we still go to watch their antics.

In 1915, several hundred people crowded the downtown streets to watch "Human Fly" George Stewart and his slide for life. On Thursday, he climbed the county courthouse using only his hands. He attached a rope to the top of the courthouse, over four hundred feet above the ground. He then dropped it to the ground, climbed down and took the rope to the Bradley Building two and half blocks away. He attached it to the roof of that four-story building. His act was to slide down the rope from the courthouse to the Bradley Building.

That night as the crowds began to gather, he climbed the side of the courthouse, placed himself in a small triangular tray and pushed off the roof. The local band struck up music to accompany this feat of daring. Cheers filled the air. To the amazement of the crowd, he flew through the air, landing on the roof of the Bradley Building. His daredevil feat left Wabash citizens dumbfounded. Word spread throughout the community of this amazing slide for life. On Friday night, he repeated the act successfully for an even larger crowd. On Saturday, it was to be a repeat performance. Thousands were eager to see this amazing act. During the day it had rained, dampening the spirit of the crowd. But Stewart was ready. He climbed up the courthouse, got in the tray and took off. Unfortunately, the rope had loosened because of the weather, and he had failed to check its tauntess. In sight of the crowd below, he hit the brick wall of the building and fell to his death on the street below.

This tragedy did not deter daredevils from coming to Wabash. Still, another daredevil event is credited to a former Wabash man also known

The Bradley Building was located on the southwest corner of Canal and Wabash Streets. It was a very popular drugstore in Wabash. In 1915, the Human Fly fell to his death while performing a stunt called the slide for life at this building. *Author's collection.*

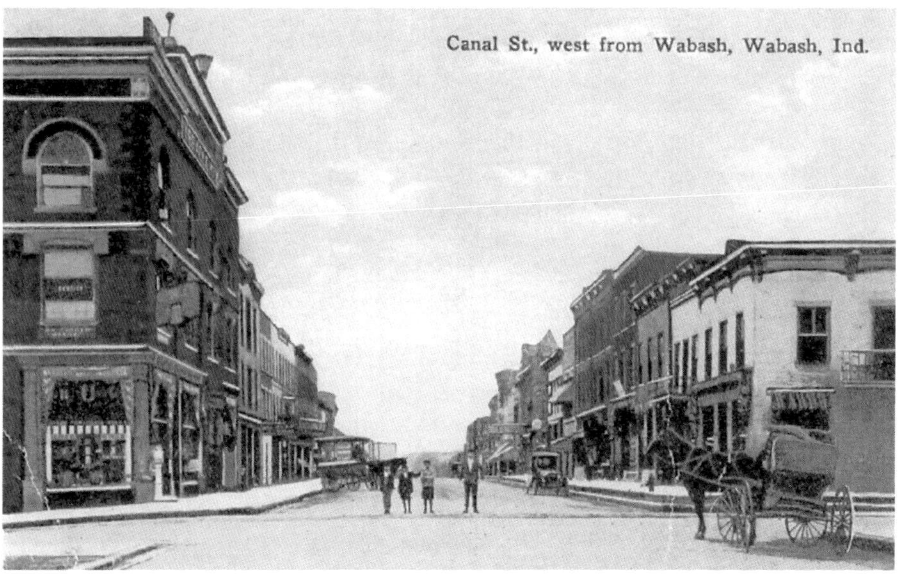

Another view of the Bradley Building. It was a stop on the streetcar line, and many people awaited the streetcar's arrival while drinking sodas at the soda fountain inside. *Author's collection.*

as the "Human Fly," Henry Roland. He performed amazing feats for nine years throughout the United States. He even had a manager named W.E. Brickman. Roland climbed the northeast corner of the Indiana Hotel at 7:30 p.m. on May 26, 1924. He had permission from the hotel and city officials to perform air stunts. Roland was quoted as saying he "liked the work." Fortunately, everything went off as expected. Such was the life of a human fly.

Gene Stratton Porter: Author, Naturalist and Photographer

Gene Stratton Porter, the daughter of Mark and Mary (Shallenberger) Stratton, was born on August 17, 1863. She spent her childhood in northern Lagro Township between Hopewell and Elko. The family house was a way station on the Underground Railroad, as her father helped fugitive slaves escape northward. It was on the 240-acre family farm that she developed her lifelong interest in and love of the outdoors, which she incorporated into her books and nature studies. She was particularly fascinated by the birds that lived on her father's farm, even nursing a chicken hawk back to life. Much of this fascination with birds she wrote about in her books *Homing with the Birds* and *What I Have Done with Birds*. One summer, when she was nearly ten years old, she "located sixty nests, and I dropped food into the open beaks in every one of them. Soon the old birds became so accustomed to me, and so convinced of my good intentions, that they would alight on my head and shoulder." Her favorite playmates were Bobby, a bantam rooster, and Hezekiah, a blue jay.

Hopewell was a small crossroads community consisting of a church, a school, a blacksmith shop, a post office, residences and a store. By far, the Hopewell Church was the center of Hopewell social life. Methodists began holding services in the area sometime before 1843, and by 1872, they had built a substantial brick church at a cost of $2,575 that is still standing. Porter's father preached at this church. It was proposed that the church be named Stratton after him, but he asked that it be called Hopewell after his British ancestors. Porter's mother and father—as well as her brother, Leander, better known as "Laddie," and her two sisters—are buried in the cemetery that surrounds the church. She wrote about several of the graves located in this cemetery.

Above: The second cabin home of Gene Stratton Porter at Wildflower Woods on Sylvan Lake near Rome City. She gave the home and land to the State of Indiana as a preserve before her death. *Courtesy of Wikipedia.*

Right: A mature Gene Stratton Porter making a point. She was dedicated to the naturalist movement. *Author's collection.*

Mark Stratton, Gene's father, preached at this small brick edifice known as the Hopewell Church, which was located in the small crossroads community of Hopewell north of Lagro. Members of the Stratton family are buried here. The church figured prominently in several of her books. *Author's collection.*

The Stratton family moved to Wabash in 1874, a move that Porter found very hard to accept. She attended grade school at the Miami Elementary School, where she did form some lifelong friendships. She found school difficult and challenging and soon dropped out. At a Chautauqua school held on Sylvan Lake near Rome City, she met her future husband, Charles D. Porter. They were married on April 21, 1886. Her marriage to Charles D. Porter led to a measure of financial security and independence for her. This allowed her to begin writing and studying nature. The couple settled at the Limberlost Cabin in Geneva, and it was here that her first short story, "Laddie, the Princess, and the Pie," was published in 1901 in *Metropolitan* magazine. Her daughter gave her as a Christmas present a camera, "a little four by four Vive which cost ten dollars." With the camera and an assistant to help and watch over her, she conducted extensive field research in the swamps, woods and meadows surrounding Limberlost.

In 1912, Gene bought property on Sylvan Lake, near Rome City, and began work on a new Limberlost Cabin. This new cabin was

A young, independent Gene Stratton Porter. She was married to Charles D. Porter, and they had one daughter, Jeannette. Jeannette later wrote a biography of her life. *Courtesy of Wikipedia.*

finished, and she moved into it in 1915. This area was named Wildflower Woods. In 1923, Gene offered Wildflower Woods to the State of Indiana as a state bird and wildflower preserve. Today, the property is home to the Gene Stratton Porter State Historic Site, where her life and accomplishments are memorialized.

In 1917, Paramount Studies produced the movie *Freckles* (1904) from the book of the same name. In 1921, her novel *Michael O'Halloran* (1915) was made into a movie by filmmaker Thomas Ince. Porter became one of the top five filmmakers of the 1920s. In January 1924, she started her own movie production company, which was cut short by her death when her limousine and a trolley car collided in Los Angeles on December 6, 1924.

Gene Stratton Porter reached a worldwide audience, estimated at fifty million readers. She sold more books between 1910 and 1924 than any other American writer. One of her most popular books was *Laddie* (1913), a novel based on the life of her brother, who drowned in the Wabash River at Lagro. Other novels she was known for were *Song of the Cardinal* (1903), *A Girl of the Limberlost* (1909), *The Harvester* (1911), *Daughter of the Land* (1918) and *The White Flag* (1923).

JOCKO ON THE LOOSE

Wabash seems to have a love affair with monkeys. At the intersection of Pike Street and Yankee Road is a section of Wabash called Monkeytown. Once, a wagon broke down there carrying monkeys to Peru. In order to pay for repairs, the owner paid his blacksmith bill with a monkey show for the entire town. The show remained in the collective memory of those in the area, hence the name Monkeytown.

For years, people have talked of seeing a pack of wild monkeys living in Falls Cemetery. Falls Cemetery used to be more wooded than it is today. People claimed those trees were full of monkeys that would follow Charley Creek down into the park for food and fun. At night, people walking through the cemetery would claim to be accosted by the creatures. They would pelt passersby with pinecones and other objects. Sometimes at night, they would start caterwauling, disturbing those in the area. In 1977, the skeleton of what looked like a monkey was found frozen in the ice at the falls of Charley Creek. Several people gathered and called in experts to look at the skeleton and determine if it was a Falls Cemetery monkey. No conclusion was reached; some thought it was truly a monkey, while others thought it was an opossum.

In 1910, Jocko, an African monkey, was exhibited in Wabash by a traveling carnival. On the last night of the carnival, as the attractions were preparing to leave, Jocko made a successful dash for freedom. As he was being transferred from his cage to a shipping crate, Jocko took advantage of the opportunity and, in the blink of an eye, was scampering across the Carroll Street Park with a keeper in hot pursuit. Fortunately for Jocko, he was able to scamper over the high board fence while the attendant was compelled to run some distance to the nearest gate.

Reaching Carroll Street, Jocko ran south until he reached the river. Then down the bank he went, jumping and chattering. He didn't stop until he came to the tall timber west of the old iron Vernon Street Bridge. The place was just as inviting as he might wish, and he was soon ensconced in the forks of a tall sycamore, where he slept until morning.

At dawn, he came down and foraged around a bit for breakfast. After satisfying his appetite, he took a plunge in the Wabash and then ran back up a towering tree, where he jumped from limb to limb and swung from tree to tree with the aid of his tail, chattering while his masters were busy taking down the tents and loading up.

Jocko was seen several times and was watched by a number of people as he swam the river three or four times. The handler never could get Jocko down or catch him. His handler gave up, and the carnival left town. Jocko

Bridge No. 509, spanning the Wabash River at Carroll and Smith Streets. *Courtesy of the Library of Congress.*

stayed. As long as there was warm weather, he was spotted all over town but particularly near the tall sycamores along the Wabash River. He continued his swims in the river, much to the amazement of kids and grownups. As winter came on, he was seldom seen and eventually disappeared. Did he find a warm home somewhere up Charley Creek and start the rumors of monkeys in Falls Cemetery? Did he find his way to Peru and the circus quarters? We will never know.

Part IV

Forgotten People, Businesses and Industry

Jones Funeral Home

Mark Jones established an undertaking firm in 1868. He had been in the lumber business, operating a sawmill and a small furniture factory in South Wabash. In 1885, the Jones and Whitcraft factory began production off Pike Street. In 1891, it organized the stock company Jones, Whitcraft and Company and erected a new stone factory building on the northeast corner of Vernon and Chestnut Streets. During the 1893 Chicago World's Fair, this factory made thousands of cheap bedroom sets for use in temporary hotels and boardinghouses in the Chicago area. By 1896, thirty men were employed in the manufacture of medium-grade furniture, which was shipped throughout northern Indiana, Ohio and Illinois. In 1896, the factory started specializing in interior house finishing work, which proved quite profitable.

W.P. Jones, Mark's son, entered the undertaking business with his father in 1878 on South Wabash Street, next to the Wabash County Bank. In 1879, W.P. moved the business to Canal Street and, later, to East Market Street, where today's Wabash County Historical Museum stands. In 1881, the *Wabash Plain Dealer* carried the following description of the business:

> *There is no branch of business more essential to the living than that which takes care of the dead…to know relatives and friends are properly cared for in their last resting place on earth, is at least gratifying, if sad…whether*

> *they be rich or poor—it is a fact that all have to pass through the hands of the undertaker as the last of earth. How much more pleasant it is to remember that the dead were laid away by proper hands...Mr. Jones commenced in the business some three years ago. He had added from time to time all the improvements in his business, such as cooling boards, improved embalming process and improved ice-boxes* [sic], *until now his establishment ranks as one of the foremost in North Indiana. He keeps a full line of caskets and coffins of all kinds...He also carries a large assortment of shrouds, undertaking trimmings, etc., all of which he is prepared to furnish on short notice and at terms and prices to suit everybody. Mr. Jones is an extensive dealer in all kinds of furniture. He handles parlor suits, bedroom sets, and all kinds of library and office furniture...He makes a specialty of fine furniture and fancy chairs...Mr. Jones has been connected with the business he follows for eleven years.*

Jones's furniture store also sold rugs, carpets, fine crystal and imported chinaware, such as Spode, Edgewood and Rosenthal.

By 1904, W.P. Jones Furniture and Undertaking was located in the Big Four Department Store building that now houses the Wabash County Historical Museum. A third generation, Homer M. "Pete" Jones, joined the family firm in 1905. At the time, Jones Funeral Home and its competition were using horse-drawn coaches. In 1916, the Jones family bought the first motorized hearse in Wabash County, a gray McFarland made in Connersville.

Before 1910, most funerals were held in the deceased's home. W.P. Jones recalled that when anyone died, "the undertaker would put a crepe on the door to show that someone had died...The crepe told the neighbors before it was in the local newspapers." He further recalled, "In the early days of the funeral business bodies were always embalmed in the home of the deceased. The undertaker had portable equipment he took to the home. He would take the casket to the house a day or so before the funeral or even later."

Another story that W.P. used to tell was of a "preacher who only preached an hour and apologized for having a short sermon."

The funeral home was moved to West Market Street where the Market Street Grill is presently located. In 1927, Homer Jones moved the business to the corner of Hill and Miami Streets. Originally known as W.P. Jones and Sons Undertaking, it became Jones Funeral Home when Homer took over the business. Homer was known as one who appreciated a joke, regardless of whether it was on himself or someone else. The biggest joke he ever played was on his brother in Pennsylvania when he sent him an old casket as a birthday present through express mail.

Homer's son, John Preston (J.P.), joined the firm and was a partner with his father for thirty-five years. He was still associated with the firm in 1976. In 1959, Homer's grandson, Stephen, joined the business, assuming ownership in 1963.

Between 1963 and 1964, the funeral home underwent extensive remodeling. Detailed record books covering decades, numerous newspaper clippings, notes and photographs were saved. On the wall in Jones's cherry-paneled office hung two pictures from 1908. One showed a high-wheeled wooden coach, the first "ambulance" in Wabash County, in front of the East Market Street address. The other photograph showed a funeral procession on West Hill Street, with four of the Jones Funeral Home's horse-drawn hearses passing Memorial Hall. Two of the hearses were black and two were white. According to Jones, "In those days men were carried in black hearses, women in white ones." Ranks of pallbearers, somber-faced, walk beside the coaches.

A large oil portrait of Homer Jones hung on the wall behind the desk. The family also saved some of the lamps from those early funeral coaches, as well as some signs that once hung on the buildings.

Steve Jones saw many changes in the undertaking business. He remembered that when his grandfather Homer "went to school to get his license, the course was two months long." When he studied at Indiana College of Mortuary Science, it took a year to complete the work.

Another change has seen funeral homes going out of the ambulance service business. The sick and injured were once picked up in horse-drawn coaches. Since 1968, funeral homes have stopped ambulance service, the business being assumed by the City of Wabash.

"The modern funeral home has taken on added responsibilities in assisting a family when a death occurs," said Jones. "There is much paperwork and many arrangements to be made, for the funeral itself, for burial sites, contacting the minister, pallbearers and others who serve a funeral."

And changing times have relieved those in the business of a somehow morbid title; they're no longer called "undertakers" but are now known as "funeral directors."

In 1981, Stephen Jones closed the Jones Funeral Home, which was the oldest in Wabash County at the time. The Jones Furniture Company was one of the businesses selected to be included in the mural on the east wall of the old Lutz Hotel facing the Tremont parking lot on Market Street.

Diehl Machines

George M. Diehl came to Peru from Chicago sometime before 1906. He was superintendent of the Mallman Addograph Company of Chicago, Illinois, in the Oakdale section of Peru. The Mallman family was from Sheboygan, Wisconsin, as was Diehl. By 1908, the company, which made adding machines and metal embossing equipment, hit hard times and sold the factory to Diehl. The Diehl Machine Company was founded in Peru, Indiana, in January 1908.

By 1909, the company employed about fifteen men with a payroll of $1,000 a month. The company had contracts to make cylinders, fly wheels, cylinder rings and value stems for automobiles, as well as a steady trade making and repairing dies for cutting and forming machinery of various kinds. A large contract had come its way, and it was looking to expand, as the Peru location was too small to carry on its work. Wabash promoter Charles Latchem, an investor in the company, saw this as an opportunity to attract it to Wabash. By September 18, 1909, Latchem was actively trying to get the company to come to Wabash, offering it incentives to make the move. Over the next several days, Latchem called for a public meeting of people interested in getting the company to move to Wabash. He also garnered the support of the *Wabash Plain Dealer* and the Wabash Exchange—a group of Wabash citizens interested in promoting Wabash. They offered the company $15,000 to come to Wabash. The Commercial Club of Peru attempted to encourage the company to stay and offered to help find a new location in the downtown area. Diehl chose Wabash.

Through the efforts of the Wabash Exchange, over two hundred Wabash citizens raised over $13,000 to entice the company to move to Wabash. The $13,000 was used to build a factory for Diehl. After the company's payroll had paid out $75,000, it would be given the property. The funds were collected at Neil Lumaree's office at 19 West Market Street. At that time, Lumaree was selling insurance and real estate. One Wabash man, Ed Bridges, walked in one morning, wrote his John Hancock on a check and put $250 down for the project. Others followed suit, and the money was raised. Businessmen of all walks of life, faiths and creeds joined together to raise the necessary capital.

By October 6, 1909, twenty-eight workers had begun constructing the factory at the northeastern intersection of Lafontaine and Wabash Streets. The stone for the building came from the Bridge family's South Side quarry. The intention was to have a well-lighted building with baths, clean washrooms

George M. Diehl moved his machine shop from Peru to this location on South Wabash Street in 1910. Originally making cogs for automobiles, he expanded the business and gained an international reputation. Diehl built a swimming pool for the community and, in the basement of his business, rented space to other companies, including Ford Meter Box and Temple Industries. *Author's collection.*

"and such other arrangements as will make…work really enjoyable." The substantial building was forty by two hundred feet; the second story was twelve feet above the basement. The gables were nine feet tall. The large timbers on which the second floor rests are solid even to this day. The roof was covered with slate. The basement was entirely cemented. The entire factory used electricity instead of steam for power.

Offices ran along eighteen feet of the west end of the building. There were three offices; the first was a general office and waiting room, the second was a private office for the transaction of business and the third was a draftsman's office where the drawings were made. A vault was installed in the southwest corner of the building. By January 1910, most of the machinery was in the factory. The factory cost $11,745 in material and labor.

By February 11, 1910, the company had completed its move to Wabash and incorporated as G.M. Diehl Machine Works, Incorporated. It occupied approximately eight hundred square feet of floor space and employed four people. Its primary business consisted of the manufacture of the Diehl Gauge, grinding machines, cutters, tools, dies and stampings. Within a short time, Diehl's employed twenty skilled men, and their output sold throughout the United States and Canada. Unfortunately, there was a shortage of skilled men to work the equipment. Workers had to be brought in from Wisconsin and Ohio, and a few followed the factory from Peru. Officers for the company were George M. Diehl, president; August Diehl, vice-president and secretary; and Charles Latchem, treasurer. By 1912, Amy D. Brannin had become the secretary of the organization, and Jessie M. Diehl (Frank's wife) was the vice-president and treasurer. Frank Diehl served as a traveling salesman for the company for a number of years.

In January 1911, the Ford Meter Box Company, which had just moved from Hartford City, shared one-third of the factory space in the front basement. In 1914, Elmer McKelrey sold Edwin Ford on the idea of starting a brass foundry in the back end of the Diehl basement. By the end of 1915, Ford Meter Box had moved its office and factory to Factory and Carroll Streets.

In 1918, the company expanded its operation and became engaged in the manufacture of woodworking machinery. The Wabash Cabinet Company used many of Diehl's products. In March 1923, Diehl made a trip through the southern United States, where he picked up contracts for $40,000 worth of machinery in Virginia furniture factories. In 1924, R.J. Lowell was appointed vice-president, and by this time, Brannin had become secretary and treasurer.

In 1937, Fred A. Collinge joined the company and, after the death of G.M. Diehl on April 21, 1938, assumed the presidency. During World War II, the company was awarded an Ordnance Pennet for its work in the war effort. By 1946, Collinge had acquired a 50 percent interest in Indian Foundry, located in Muncie, Indiana. In 1949, the company bought the rights to the

As demand for Diehl's machinery grew, the factory purchased the old canning factory that sat behind it, and by 1950, Diehl's had expanded its original factory by incorporating the canning factory into its operation. *Author's collection.*

Vonnegut molder. By 1950, the company occupied 100,000 square feet and had 125 people in its employ. During the 1950s, it developed a line of gang rip saws (SL52), began marketing a new type of tapeless splicer and bought the Bradley automatic turning lathe. This machine turned out table and chair legs, gunstocks, bowling pins and so on. In 1955, Wallace E. Carroll, a Chicago industrialist, purchase G.M. Diehl Machine Works, Incorporated. John Collinge remained as president, but C.W. Tuttle was appointed executive vice-president in 1958. In early 1960, Collinge retired, and Tuttle became president.

By 1976, Diehl's employed seventy people, manufacturing high-production woodworking machinery. In 1981, it was a division of Waltham Watch Company, a subsidiary of Katy Industries Incorporated. By 1993, Diehl Machines was a division of Hallmark Holdings, Incorporated, with Robert F. Rozman as president. Despite the decline in the use of wood in the manufacture of cabinetry and furniture, Diehl Machines has continued to find foreign and domestic markets for its quality-made Wabash products.

"Wabash" George Mullin

"Wabash" George Mullin, a right-handed pitcher in Major League Baseball, was born in Toledo, Ohio, on July 4, 1880, to Martin and Nellie (Kelly) Mullin. He was brought to Wabash in 1899 by Milo Meredith to pitch in what was called the Two-Eye League. It was while playing semipro ball in Wabash that he earned the nickname "Wabash" George. At that time, the baseball games were played on South Carroll Street just north of the river. On December 24, 1900, he married Grace Aukerman. In 1901, he was with the Fort Wayne Western Association and highly regarded. In August, the Boston American Association tried to get him, offering a salary of $1,900 and a bonus of $250. He replied that he would accept a salary of $2,000 and a bonus of $300. He was also in touch with American League (AL) managers in Detroit, Cleveland and Chicago. Mullin signed with both the Brooklyn Superbas and the Detroit Tigers. Wishing to stay close to home, he chose the Tigers. He played fourteen total seasons with the Detroit Tigers (1902–13), Washington Senators (1913) and Indianapolis Hoosiers/Newark Pepper (1914–15).

Wabash George had a large following in Wabash, where he lived during the off-season. For many years, one of the earliest signs of spring in Wabash

County was Wabash George Mullin heading south for spring training. The Detroit Tigers did their training at various places, one of which was Hot Springs, Arkansas.

Wabash George was a powerfully built right-hander who had an intimidating fastball but had imperfect control. He would keep opposing batters off balance by talking to them, or just talking to himself, when they came to bat. He compiled a career record of 228-196, ranking sixty-fifth in wins in major-league history. He had remarkable stamina as a pitcher. He started 428 games and had 353 complete games—the twenty-fifth highest total in major-league history. He was among the American League leaders in complete games from 1903 to 1911 and innings pitched from 1903 to 1910. His career highs were 42 completed games (1904) and 382 $^1/_3$ innings (1905).

In his rookie year, he started out slow. The Detroit Club did not make use of him in the pitcher's box as expected. However, Wabash George won thirteen games and lost sixteen for the seventh-place Tigers. The following season, he won nineteen and reduced his ERA to 2.25. That same year, he had six shutouts (second in the AL) and 170 strikeouts (fifth in the AL) and played in forty-one games (second in the AL).

From 1907 to 1909, the Tigers won the American League Pennant. Mullin won 66 games and pitched 105 complete games and more than 950 innings. His best season was in 1909, when he started the season with a one-hitter on opening day and then recorded twelve consecutive wins. He did not lose a game until June 15, 1909, when he lost to the Philadelphia Athletics. He went on to lead the AL in both wins (29) and win percentage (.784). He started in 6 World Series games. He gave up only twelve earned runs in 58 innings, for a lifetime ERA of 1.86 in World Series play. During his time with the Detroit Tigers, he established a record, which has not been broken, of pitching 34 innings in the 1909 World Series.

In November 1909, he toured Cuba with a group of Detroit Tigers playing twelve exhibition games against the Cuban teams of Habana and Alemendares. The Tigers lost eight of the twelve games, but on November 27, 1909, Wabash George shut out the Alemndares in a 4–0 victory for the Tigers.

He teamed with such Tiger stars as Donovan, Bush, Crawford, Schaeffer, O'Leary, McIntyre and Ty Cobb. On September 18, 1909, Wabash George pinch hit for Ty Cobb in the bottom of the ninth inning and hit a triple into center field.

One of the greatest thrills of his life came on his thirty-first birthday when he pitched a no-hitter game against the St. Louis Browns. Another was when President Teddy Roosevelt invited him to the White House for supper.

On April 20, 1912, he was given the honor of pitching the first game at the new Navin Field, where he beat the Indians 6–5 in eleven innings. That same year on July 4, he pitched the first no-hitter in Detroit Tigers history. In May 1913, he left Detroit for the Washington Nationals. He worked hard and conscientiously, but for some reason, his former cunning had deserted him. He admitted that he was not pitching the kind of ball to warrant his retention in the Major Leagues. The manager called him in and said, "I am sorry, George, but I will have to let you go. I offer you a choice of cities and managers. Buffalo or Rochester, both of whom are willing to take you off my hands."

In 1914, Wabash George went to the newly formed Federal League and played for the Indianapolis Hoosiers. There, he pitched twenty-three games, winning eleven and losing twelve. He was hitting near the three hundred mark. He "won a warm place in the hearts of Indiana fandom by his brilliant slab work and timely hitting." In 1915, the Hoosiers moved east and became the Newark Pepper. He played only five games with them, and his last major-league game was on May 23, 1915.

During his baseball career, Wabash George sustained many injuries. In 1901, while playing at Fort Wayne, he pitched several innings effectively and lined out a two-sacker but injured his shoulder, causing it to swell. He could not play for two weeks and missed a game against Toledo. In 1912, he was out for five to six weeks for a herniated disc; in 1913, he was out for two to three weeks for a strained bicep tendon; in 1915, he was out for five weeks for a ruptured elbow ligament; in 1917, he was out for five weeks for a broken finger; and in 1918, he was out for five weeks for a broken hand and, five months later, for one to two weeks for a pulled elbow ligament. The workhorse was tiring out.

Wabash George retired from baseball and lived in Wabash. For a time, he tended bar at the Elks Lodge. He was a member of St. Bernard's Church and the Elks and the Maccabees Lodges in Wabash. He lived the rest of his life at 463 North Cass Street, dying on January 7, 1944, after four weeks of serious illness. He is buried in Falls Cemetery. He was posthumously inducted into the Michigan Sports Hall of Fame in 1962.

An Illustrated History of the Wabash Sweet Shop

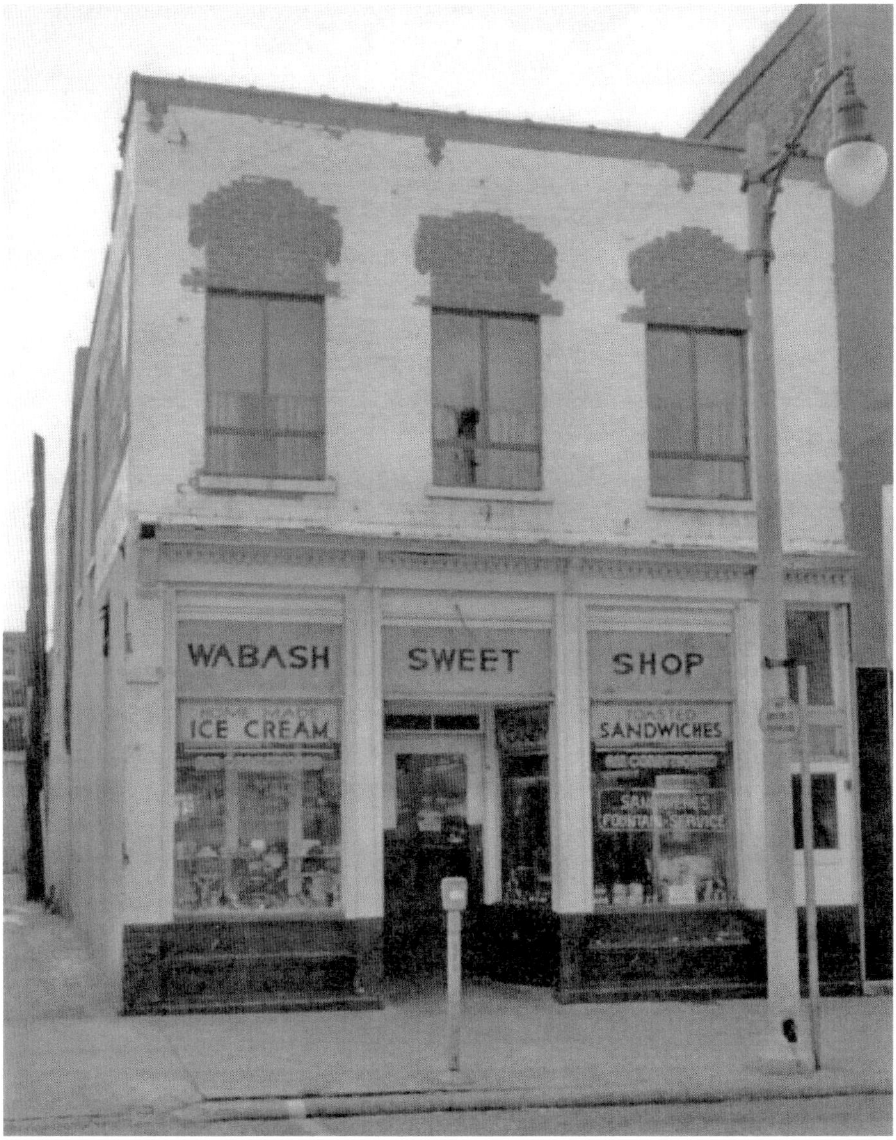

John Morris, an immigrant from Greece, and his wife opened the Wabash Sweet Shop in 1938 in a building that had previously been a tavern. The store became famous for its chocolate candy made from recipes developed by John. *Author's collection.*

John Morris developed a recipe for ice cream that was very popular for many years. The ice cream was made in the back of the store and sold over the counter in cones, sundaes, shakes and malts. You could also buy it in cartons to take home. Many of the young people of the community remember going to the Eagles Theater for the Saturday matinee and afterward stopping in the Sweet Shop to get a butterscotch milkshake. You got a glassful and the metal mixer cup as well to refill. *Author's collection.*

People always loved the hustle and bustle of the Sweet Shop. John Morris never had a ticket line for orders. The waitress would holler out your order. The shop, a longtime Wabash landmark, was remodeled several times, and most people remember it as shown here. In 2001, the owners, Conrad and Diane Morris, closed the store. *Author's collection.*

BOB PRINTY

Robert N. Printy, the son of Everette F. and Ruth R. (Biggerstaff) Printy, was born on August 11, 1901. He was the eldest of three children. Printy grew up in Lagro and attended the local schools but did not graduate from Lagro High School. He had other plans.

Early in his life, he became interested in what was called "catch wrestling," made popular by Martin "Farmer" Burns. Catch wrestling was popular in carnivals and circuses in the late nineteenth and early twentieth centuries. Catch wrestlers like Printy would challenge locals as part of the athletic show. If a local could defeat a wrestler, also called a strongman, he won a cash prize as well as bragging rights. Like many other wrestlers, Printy had some wrestling skills he had learned in school and joined a show to escape the humdrum life on the farm.

In 1923, Bob Printy was with the Jack Reynolds wrestling team. In the 1920s, Jack Reynolds was the champion welterweight wrestler of the world. He was recognized as the fastest grappler in the game. At the age of thirteen, Reynolds was told he had tuberculosis and would not live long, but he refused to give up. He was also coach of the Indiana University wrestling team. In April 1923, Printy was featured in a wrestling bout at the Lagro gym. An exhibition match was put on with Arthur Rhamy right before a basketball game between the teachers of Lagro High School and the hack drivers. Printy lost the six-minute match when Rhamy threw him into a body scissors move. Printy was also working with a wrestler by the name of Held, who was the Indiana welterweight champion. By 1924, he was the manager of Tommy Tucker's road tour, where Tucker wrestled at fairs in southwestern Ohio. Printy also wrestled, winning matches and losing one. In April 1925, Printy wrestled in Wabash for the first time. He took second billing to the popular Wabash High School coach Billy Thom. He left a very favorable impression on the community. The newspaper described the 175-pound wrestler as "fast and strong as the proverbial bull." His first match was held in the WAA Community Gym. Later, he began to assist Coach Thom in coaching the Wabash High School wrestling team. In August 1927, Printy was wrestling in Texas with Thom and doing well.

By 1930–31, Printy was under the big top, performing as an athletic act with the Sparks Circus and, later, with the Sells-Floto Circus. For his act, he would demonstrate wrestling moves and wrestle all takers. He also served as a strongman. In 1934, he was with the Barnes Circus.

Bob Printy was very popular with the other performers in the circus. After Printy's death, the circus train would stop on the tracks at Lagro to honor him. Here, he holds two other performers from the circus. Bob performed as an athletic act, usually as a wrestler. *Courtesy of John Lawson.*

Bob Printy, always gregarious by nature, met a lot of people while performing in the circus. Here Bob is holding cowboy star Tom Mix's daughter, Thomasina (Tommy). *Courtesy of John Lawson.*

According to a circus magazine, the *Billboard*, in January 1941, Printy was a defense guard in California. In September 1942, the following appeared in the same magazine: "Bob Printy former circus wrestler and for the past 20 months a defense guard, writes that he enlisted in the Navy and will be attached to its physical staff. Recently he visited Cole, Lewis Mills and King circuses."

On January 23, 1943, Printy was assigned to NCTC Camp Bradford undergoing, "physical training and combat staff [*sic*]." Sometime while in the service, he played roles in Hollywood movies that were made for servicemen.

Among Bob Printy's collection of photographs is this picture of cowboy actor Tom Mix. Printy and Mix were both with the Sells-Floto Circus from 1929 to 1931. The woman dressed in western attire in the picture is Mix's wife. *Courtesy of John Lawson.*

Tom Mix (1880–1940) and his third wife, Victoria Forde, standing in front of a Sells-Floto wagon with other unidentified circus employees. Mix was a film star of early westerns, appearing in 291 films. In 1927, he was the number one box office star. From 1929 to 1931, he appeared in the Sells-Floto Circus at a salary reported at $20,000. *Courtesy of John Lawson.*

One role he played was that of a captured serviceman. The Germans would then hang him from a tree. "A rope is tied to a tree, and around the wrestler's neck, and he drops something like 40 feet, and it doesn't break his neck." His neck was so muscular that it did not hurt him. This was called the "hangman's drop," made famous by Farmer Burns, an early wrestler. Although in the navy,

Printy found an occasional match. On July 9, 1943, Printy wrestled Johnny Marrs at the Oakland stadium with a crowd of four thousand in attendance. The match ended in a draw as the time limit had expired.

By October 24, 1944, Printy was stationed in San Diego. The November 21, 1944 *Wabash Keewanus Bullaton* mentions that Bob Printy was in San Diego and had visited with Harry J. Hutchens at 11541 Chiquita Street in North Hollywood, California. Harry's wife, Jane, was Marjorie Stewart's sister.

On January 9, 1945, Homer Showalter reported in the *Bullaton*:

> *They tell me that Glazier and Printy are getting together with Harry J. Hutchens out in Hollywood, Cal. Also that Printy the old judo instructor in San Diego may ship out one of these days. Would I hate to be the Japs that that boy gets hold of. I well remember the first time he and Coach Thom tangled here in Wabash. I guess they never get old in the wrestling game.*

On January 16, 1945, Bob Printy was given leave and returned to Wabash County. He visited with Showalter in his office. Showalter reported that he was "still a Judo instructor in California with Charles Glazier and Bob was telling me something about a widow lady that he knew out there, but I better not mention it, I guess. My Judo is a little rusty, since Coach Thom left Wabash." Later that week, he said:

> *Printy of wrestling fame breezed into the office here Saturday all full of steam and big talk, and incidentally mentioned a certain widow out in Calif. Now, Harry Williams, the big stock and truck man of Lagro tells me that the scuttle butte* [sic] *has it around Lagro, that wily old Bob is already married to the lovely widow. Coach Thom will get a kick out of this. Can you imagine Printy being married.*

On June 5, 1945, Showalter reported:

> *The old wrestler Bob Printy is now out for good, after instructing in Judo for about 3½ years. They tell me that Bob had a show of Judo tactics the boys put on that sold more War Bonds than Hedy Lamarr, Bob Hope and the rest of them combined. Incidentally Bob doesn't know whether he will stay here in good old Indiana or not, as he has a good job offered him in Calif., and confidentially, a little widow out there that carries an awful wallop with Bob. This is just between us as I don't believe Bob wants anything said about it.*

In November 1951, Printy married Dorothy L. Jacobs in Wabash County and settled down to a more peaceful life in Lagro. He worked at Celotex until he retired and was active in the Tuscan Masonic Lodge of Lagro. Occasionally, when a circus train went through Lagro, it would slow down in honor of Printy. He enjoyed staying in touch with his many circus friends and sharing his collection of circus photographs. He would often drive into Wabash and spend the morning with Kenneth "Bill" Gray at the museum, sharing stories and experiences he had gathered over the years, but he delighted particularly in stories about Coach Thom. Dorothy died on July 29, 1974, at the age of fifty-nine and was buried in the Lagro IOOF Cemetery. Printy died on December 31, 1981, at Stephenson's Supermarket in Lagro. He was buried next to his wife, father and mother.

THE WABASH HIGH SCHOOL TICKET BOOTH

By 1932, nearly fifteen million people were unemployed throughout the United States. For the people of Wabash County, the effects of the long economic slump were all too real. It brought a multitude of problems, including unemployment, bank failure and factory closings.

The Wabash City Council made drastic budget cuts late in 1932 and continued to hack away at expenses. It cut the number of street lamps in the downtown area nearly in half and ordered the remaining lights turned off at eleven o'clock each night. It reduced garbage collections from once a week to once every two weeks and threatened to direct the police department to park its only patrol car except in cases of extreme emergency.

As unemployment increased, the number of families on relief grew. In the summer of 1932, Mayor Homer T. Showalter hoped to find room for six hundred gardens for needy families. In January 1933, increasing numbers of children were going to school hungry. Three of the city's five grade schools began providing a hot breakfast each morning.

The Wabash Carnegie Public Library was about to shut its doors for several months because it, too, was out of money. Della Tilman, the librarian, was the library's only employee, and the library board cut her salary by 10 percent.

On March 5, 1933, one day after being sworn into office, President Franklin D. Roosevelt closed all of the nation's remaining banks. Cash all but disappeared from circulation here, and most merchants refused to accept checks.

In the spring of 1933, some three hundred men found temporary employment when county commissioners, aided by federal funds, put three hundred men to work on country roads. Each man worked ten-hour days. These men gathered each morning in front of the Hotel Indiana, where they climbed aboard open trucks to be transported to work sites.

In late November, a handful of men gathered in front of the chamber of commerce office at Miami and Market Streets. With hats pulled tightly over their heads and coat collars turned up against the chill, the men shuffled about in an effort to stay warm. They were soon joined by others until the group numbered two hundred. They had come downtown to collect their initial paychecks from the Civil Works Administration (CWA), the first public employment experiment of the New Deal. President Franklin D. Roosevelt and Harry Hopkins, FDR's relief administrator, had created the CWA only a few weeks before. George M. Diehl, a Wabash industrialist, oversaw the local efforts of the CWA, and by mid-December, more than six hundred men here were on the government's payroll. Cora Wilson supervised a smaller number of women who worked on CWA projects.

The men in the CWA program labored at a wide assortment of jobs, including painting the interiors of the county jail, the Women's Clubhouse and the county hospital. Other projects included tree trimming; county drainage ditch maintenance; street repairs in Wabash, Roann and North Manchester; and fixing county roads. Work for women included cleaning at the county home and the hospital and sewing garments for unemployed people. The pay for these jobs averaged a bit less than four dollars per day.

By the end of 1933, seven hundred men and women had found jobs through the CWA. But George Diehl was forced to cut three workers from the program because the government rules provided for only 697 jobs in the area. The government discontinued the short-lived CWA in the early spring of 1934, but within a year, Congress funded the Works Progress Association (WPA), which took over many CWA projects and created many more.

One WPA project was the construction of the Wabash High School ticket booth in 1939. In 1897, bricks had been used to pave the downtown streets. When the streets were repaved with asphalt, the bricks were salvaged. The saved bricks were then used to construct the ticket booth at the high school football field. For years afterward, it became a tradition for incoming seniors to paint the ticket booth the summer before the start of their senior year. On one side of the building was an imposing message of some sort, such as "Wabash Apaches Can Play. You can talk the game. But can you play the game?" The other side of the ticket booth was reserved for the names of the seniors who had helped paint the building. This tradition is very much alive today. Another tradition, although not always carried out, is for students of rival Northfield and Southwood High Schools to vandalize the work of the WHS seniors.

BIG FOOT ATTACKS

Very early in Wabash County history there were reports of strange creatures in the Lagro area. As late as 1980, reports circulated in that vicinity of a strange beast that prowled the woods during the day and ventured forth at night to kill cattle. In that year, a large number of sheep disappeared, which was credited to the ferocious beast. Many in and around Lagro heard weird sounds at night resembling the wail of a child with a particularly plaintive tone that makes it all the more dreadful. Parties were organized to hunt for the creature. Only once was the creature sighted—and even then, only at a distance—as it skulked along a fence in the gloom.

Since the building of the Salamonie Reservoir Dam by the United States Army Corps of Engineers, people have talked of hearing, seeing and smelling an unusual creature that roamed the area. Fishermen along the river, campers in the woods and nearby farmers have reported their dogs acting strangely and becoming suddenly afraid. Fishermen have reported that a large turtle living in the man-made lake occasionally surfaces, tipping over boats. Unusual cat screams have been heard from one end of the reservoir to the other.

Several years ago, two men were boating down the Wabash River. It was an annual weekend fishing trip for them. They had put in the river below Huntington and had been floating along, casting their lines, when they reached deep potholes in the river. It was getting late in the afternoon when they reached the area between Hanging Rock and the mouth of the Salamonie. They found a secluded spot on the south bank, set up a tent and began a fire to fry the fish they had caught that day. After eating, they hiked the short distance back to Hanging Rock and climbed to the top to survey the surrounding countryside. Around 10:00 p.m., tired from their long day, they decided to go to sleep and retired to the tent they had set up.

Fog rolled in and engulfed the area, reducing visibility. Shortly after midnight, their dog, which was sleeping between them, sat up and began to growl, waking them up. The dog quickly bolted from the tent as if

Hanging Rock was called by early explorers a "sugar loaf" because of its appearance. In reality, it was an ancient coral reef formed millions of years ago when the county was covered by a tropical sea. *Courtesy of Wikipedia.*

attacking something. Their first thought was that a raccoon was close by and had stirred up the dog. However, they heard a loud thump, and their dog came running back to camp whimpering with its tail between its legs. They also began to smell something very strong and pungent that they had not smelled before.

As they peered out of their tent, they could see very little because of the fog. But they could hear something large moving through the woods, past the tent and down to the edge of the river. The dog refused to go out of

The mouth of the Salamonie River. The Big Miami Indian Reserve began on the west bank of the river. On the east bank was the site of a Big Foot attack on a pair of camping canoers. *Author's collection.*

the tent. When whatever it was got to the riverbank, it began to throw rocks into the river and then began to throw rocks at the tent. Both men moved to the fire they had built earlier and stood there, hoping that would discourage whatever was out there. The creature began moving back toward the camp.

It began to circle the camp and the men. As it got closer, they could make out the image of something that was dark in color and covered with hair. It stood nearly eight feet tall and walked upright with amazing agility. Its arms hung at its side, and its hands reached nearly to its knees. It continued to circle them until daylight, when it disappeared.

Both men quickly took down their tent, cleaned up the site and went down to their boat to get out of there. They found their fishing boat had been dented from being tossed around on the rocks along the riverbank, and rocks were lying in the bottom where they had been thrown during the attack. They packed up the boat and took off for home. In future trips down the Wabash, they have quickly moved past this spot to find a better place.

TOMMY R. MILLER: WABASH COUNTY HERO

During the Vietnam War, Wabash County lost sixteen men. The second young man to give his life for his country was Tommy R. Miller. Miller was born on May 7, 1943, the son of Arden and Genevee Miller, and spent most of his life in the sleepy little community of Laketon, Indiana. He went to school in Laketon and graduated from Laketon High School in 1961. There were twenty-nine other people in his graduating class. He attended the United Brethren Church in Laketon.

Like many a youth in the 1960s, he had a decision to make: serve his country or find a way out of it. In January 1964, he made his decision by enlisting in the United States Navy. The recruiting office was located in Memorial Hall, one floor below the museum. There, he met with recruiting representatives of each branch of the service, who were impressive in their neat, clean uniforms. They each talked up their branch of the service and the benefits they had to offer. Miller enlisted with five other Wabash County youth—James A. Risser, John L. Butler, Mickey E. Hudson, Ronald E. Swygart and Jerry D. Flinn—all of whom were sent to San Diego for basic training. Miller, Butler, Hudson and Swygart were in the same graduating class. In basic training, Miller learned about the navy's history, customs, drills and basic seamanship, such as tying knots. He endured physical training, fighting fires and marching drills. He marched everywhere from the barracks to the chow hall to class and back to the barracks. In April, he completed basic training and was selected to become a hospital corpsman (HC).

Miller packed up his duffel bag and headed to school at Great Lakes. After graduating from Hospital Corpsman School, he was stationed at the naval air station in Point Mugu. In April 1965, Miller volunteered to go to Vietnam, serving as a hospital corpsman assigned to the Second Battalion, Fourth Marines. The motto of this outfit was "Second to None." In May 1965, the marines landed at Chu Lai, Quang Ngai Province. One marine once said of this province, "If there was one place you didn't want to be as an American serviceman it was Quang Ngai." Before long, they were involved in Operation Starlite, their first major engagement.

Operation Starlight was followed by Operation Double Eagle on January 28, 1966. It was during this operation that Miller met and struck up a friendship with another hospital corpsman, Carl Dunaway.

> *He* [Miller] *was a very likable guy and he and I, along with other corpsmen, had this fraternity, almost, that we belonged to and we took it*

> *very personal when we lost one of them...we knew each other by name on sight. In "Operation Double Eagle" we were against the People's Army of Vientnam* [PAVN] *18th Regiment, 325th Division. That operation scared everyone because the PAVN used Chinese tactics, bugles that were not done since the Korean War and they over ran us.*

Miller and Dunaway continued their friendship after Operation Double Eagle. "Our conversations were always more along the line of our job. How to do this and how to do that. I don't ever recall us talking about our life growing up or even our folks. A lot of our conversations were interrupted by gunfire and interruptions from various sergeants telling us to get up and move." As a hospital corpsman, Miller had to treat so many other

> *things than they would ever have to think of in the states. There were guys who had their toes bit off by rats while sleeping. We had some who were mauled by black panthers while on ambushes. The humidity was one of the worst factors against us. We had guys with mold and fungus which grew under their arms and crotch. I and Tommy, didn't get to sleep in a bed for probably six months. We slept on the ground. We wore the same clothes for most of that time also because we just couldn't pack several changes of clothes with us.*

On March 5, the Second Battalion and other outfits were sent on Operation Utah. It was be the first time the marines engaged the soldiers of the PAVN, particularly the Thirty-sixth Infantry Regiment of the PAVN. It was the job of the Second Battalion to establish blocking positions to close enemy escape routes. Miller was carried into this engagement on a UH-34 helicopter capable of carrying 1,600 pounds. On reaching the landing zone, the UH-34's came under heavy small arms fire. As Miller was running from the helicopter, he was shot in the head.

Dunaway was on Miller's last mission. Dunaway says of that mission:

> *We were all lifted in with these UH-34's (ugly looking helicopters)...He was on another chopper but on the same third wave.*
>
> *I remember waiting for the choppers to come back for us and it seemed like forever. When they did most of them all had many, many bullet holes in them. The chopper I boarded had a hole in its side bigger than a watermelon. I could stick my head through it if I wanted to. When we landed a firefight*

was already going on. We were, I thought, surrounded. We basically got ambushed as my diary described it. I think I was kneeling, trying to figure out which way to go when I heard someone behind me get hit. I heard my name called out, which surprised me. Before I knew it and could turn around, he [Tommy] *was thrown down on me. I thought it was just another Marine. I knew he had a head wound and* [was] *probably dead or damn close to it. I also knew there wasn't anything I could do for him. I cradled his body, you know not even knowing it was him because his face was so swollen and blue.*

The noise around me I remember was so ungodly loud. Hundreds of weapons going off at the same time along with mortars, the choppers and screaming. I pulled the man around and got him laying across my lap and searched for his dog tags. His face looked so bad. I had his blood down the back [of] *my neck, all over my left side, and covering my lap. I looked at his dog tags and at that moment, it was like the whole world went quiet. I kept looking at his face wondering who this man was. I knew it couldn't have been the same Tommy Miller I knew. But it was. I think it was a few minutes later a couple of Marines pulled me away from there. Then I saw another corpsman by the name of Lockhart get hit when he ran across a dike. The same two Marines that pulled me away from Tommy went for Lockhart and were killed. This all started about 9:00 in the morning and was still going on at 11:00 at night when we had an emergency ammo drop…Tommy never—and I mean this with my whole being—never felt a thing. He did not die like so many hundreds that I saw where they laid in pain and agony.*

We had so many Marines that were wounded that day that after we were able to get them to the [landing zone] *they bled to death because we couldn't get choppers in to pick them up. If Tommy would have only been wounded, he may still have died because there was no way of getting him out until the next day.*

On March 8, 1966, Miller's parents received a telegram informing them that he had been killed in action. His body was returned to the Bender Funeral Home in North Manchester, and he was buried in Pleasant Hill Cemetery, just west of North Manchester.

THE KIDNAPPING OF BABY JESUS

Thanksgiving morning 1991 was like any other Thanksgiving—mothers were preparing turkey with all the trimmings for their families; men were finding things to do to stay out of their wives' way; kids were enjoying their first day of vacation from school.

Mayor Dallas Winchester was looking forward to a peaceful day when the phone rang. A low, gruff voice said, "Baby Jesus is gone! We have kidnapped him from the courthouse nativity scene. We will call back with a list of demands." The caller abruptly hung up. Puzzled, Winchester called the Wabash Police Department and asked it to check into the matter. Yes, baby Jesus was missing! The city police contacted the sheriff's department, since it was their property.

At first, Winchester believed the kidnapping was done by someone who was unhappy with the nativity scene on the courthouse lawn and dismissed

For years, Wabash has had a manger scene on the courthouse lawn without any problems. However, that all changed in 1991 when baby Jesus was kidnapped and held for ransom. On Christmas Day 1991, baby Jesus was returned after being found in a ditch. Since then, baby Jesus has been wired into the manger to stop further kidnapping attempts. *Author's collection.*

it as a prank. He felt confident, as did the community, that Sheriff Bill Wheatley would recover baby Jesus.

For thirty years, the Wabash Lions Club had provided and maintained the nativity scene on the courthouse lawn. Never, in all that time, had there been a problem. "It's something we do for the spirit of Christmas for the people of the county," Lions Club secretary Phill Hall said. He and Lions Club president Rex Price were shocked to hear of the kidnapping. "I'm appalled that someone would bother doing something like that," Price said. "We've never had anything like this before. I can't understand why anyone would do this, unless it's something symbolic."

For weeks, people in the community called one another or stopped friends in stores to talk about the kidnapping of baby Jesus and possible suspects. The police were stymied, having no leads. The kidnappers remained silent. No demands were issued for baby Jesus's return. People walked by and looked at the empty crèche and shook their heads as they walked on. Children began to hear of the missing baby Jesus. But, after all, it was the Christmas season, and wonderful things happen at that time of the year.

Janet Shoemaker read the story of the kidnapping to her young children, Larissa and Mark. "When I read them that story, they were very distraught. It had far more impact on them than I thought it would." The children kept thinking about the loss of baby Jesus; to them "it was so sad." After visiting the nativity scene, the children "said that Joseph and Mary looked so sad."

"Let's put a baby in it," Larissa suggested. Their mother warned them that they might risk losing their doll, as someone had already stolen baby Jesus, but they were willing to take the risk. The children chose as their replacement a Cabbage Patch Kid given to Mark by his grandmother. Larissa wrote a note and attached it to the surrogate baby Jesus, explaining what she and her brother had done:

> *Dear Everyone,*
>
> *We know this is not the baby Jesus. It is just a baby doll, but we didn't want the crib to be empty at Christmas. We love Jesus very much especially at this time of year. We didn't steal Jesus but we want to give you this doll until you find the other Jesus.*
>
> *From Larissa and Mark Shoemaker*

They placed their doll in the crèche. As they did, Larissa asked, "I wonder if this is all right. Maybe we should go inside and ask the judge if it's OK?"

Rumors of a new baby Jesus circulated throughout town. Phill Hall and his wife went to see for themselves and found the doll, wrapped in a purple blanket, with the note attached. He was concerned that since the first baby Jesus was taken, this one would be as well. "We'll make sure the family gets their doll back," Hall said. "I think it's really neat what they did. It shows that there are caring people out there, as well as weirdoes, but the good people outnumber the others."

On Christmas Eve, the long-silent kidnappers made their demands known. The *Wabash Plain Dealer*, the mayor, the library and four "randomly selected citizens"—including Dorais Chevrolet and Ron Woodward—received ransom letters. The four-page, handwritten letter listed a host of demands. The *Plain Dealer* also received a picture of baby Jesus held captive in an animal cage. The kidnappers' demands for the release of baby Jesus were:

1. City police policemen had to start wearing hats again.
2. A certain Wabash patrolman had to get a haircut, wear glasses and walk around downtown.
3. The Christmas "eye sores" were to be left on display all year.
4. The Paradise Spring monument had to be torn down as it was an example of "hatrosity."
5. A certain Wabash doctor should wear his seatbelt and stop slouching in his car.
6. Mayor Dallas Winchester had to make certain public and embarrassing appearances on the courthouse square, including crawling on all fours and making the sounds of a pig.
7. Keep Off the Grass signs had to be removed from the courthouse lawn.
8. The courthouse clock had to be replaced.

The writers went on to say that they never meant to hurt anybody, but "one day I was driving around and I heard some people say that if I didn't take the baby, they were going to tie me up and steal my bag of magic tricks." The letter ended with "Merry Christmas!" The police department collected all copies of the letter as evidence and tried to find fingerprints.

On Christmas morning, the long ordeal came to an end when baby Jesus was recovered. An anonymous phone call to Chuck Adams at Radio WKUZ told him where baby Jesus could be found. Adams relayed the information to Wabash police, who found the figure in a cardboard box on Bailey Road near County Road 500 South.

A postcard of the Wabash courthouse. On March 31, 1880, arc lights on top of the courthouse lit up the town of Wabash, making it the first electrically lighted municipality in the world. *Author's collection.*

Sheriff Bill Wheatley said the internal evidence in the four-page letter suggested the incident might have been the work of three people. He said the department's officers had some ideas about who may have been involved. He did not see anything funny about the incident, regarding it as both sacrilegious and an act of mischief.

Mayor Winchester was "glad its over. I'm glad the baby Jesus is back." Going further, he said, "I thought it was rather stupid. I don't understand why people can't make better use of their time."

The case is probably still open, and no one has ever been brought to justice for the kidnapping of baby Jesus.

Bibliography

Cass County Commissioners Records. Cass County, Indiana.

Family Branches. Wabash County Genealogical Society, 1995–2014.

The John Tipton Papers. 2 vols. Indianapolis: Bookwalter-Ball-Greathouse, 1942.

Paul, John Peter. *We Run the Canal Line: Being the Diary of John Peter Paul, a Member of the Party Engaged in the Preliminary Survey of the Wabash & Erie Canal in the Year 1827*. Crawfordsville, IN: R.E. Banta, 1933.

Peek at the Past. Wabash County Historical Society, 2008–2014.

Scott, James, and John Scott. *The Indiana Gazetteer, Or, Topographical Dictionary: Containing a Description of the Several Counties, Towns, Villages, Settlements, Roads, Lakes, Rivers, Creeks, and Springs, in the State of Indiana*. 2nd ed. Indianapolis: Douglass and Maguire, 1833.

Wabash County Commissioners Records, 1835–present.

Wabash (IN) Plain Dealer, 1870–1920.

Wabash Weekly Gazette, September 10, 1851.

Woodward, Ronald L. "Wabash County and the Vietnam War." http://www.ingenweb.org/inwabash/vietnam-news.html. 2011.

———. *Watching Wabash Grow: Businesses of 1881*. Wabash, IN: Ronald L. Woodward, 2004.

About the Author

Ron Woodward. *Author's collection.*

Ron Woodward was born and raised in New Albany, Indiana. He graduated from Indiana University while serving in the United States Navy. After his discharge, he received his master's degree from Ball State University. He has taught in the Greater Clark County school system, the Muncie school system and Wabash City Schools. He has also taught at the Upper Wabash Vocational School and a methods class at Manchester College. He has served as president of the Wabash County Historical Society and the Wabash County Genealogical Society, which he helped to form.

He has been honored as Indiana Geography Teacher of the Year and Wal-Mart Teacher of the Year, named 2000 Hosier Historian by the Indiana Historical Society and was a semifinalist Indiana Teacher of the Year. He was named Wabash Distinguished Citizen of the Year for 2013. He has served as Wabash County historian since 1981 and was a sponsor of the Indiana Junior Historical Society Club for twenty-five years.